THE STRANGEST
AIRCRAFT
OF ALL TIME

THE STRANGEST
AIRCRAFT
OF ALL TIME

KEITH RAY

The
History
Press

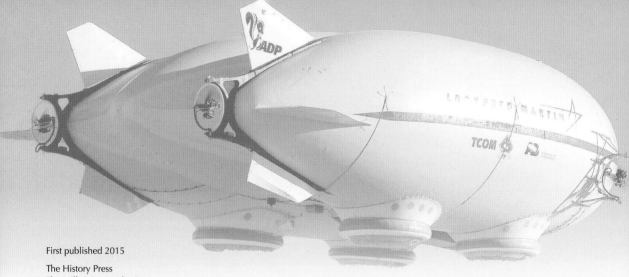

First published 2015

The History Press
The Mill, Brimscombe Port
Stroud, Gloucestershire, GL5 2QG
www.thehistorypress.co.uk

British Library Cataloguing in Publication Data.
A catalogue record for this book is available from the British Library.

ISBN 978 0 7509 6097 7

Typesetting and origination by The History Press
Printed in China

CONTENTS

During my RAF basic flying training at RAFC Cranwell I remember going to an RAF station, somewhere in the Wiltshire area, Hullavington I seem to recall, to meet up with the RAF rugby team for a training session. We were playing someone like Lydney that evening and a carload of us were travelling down from the Midlands. As we drove in through the main gate I saw an aircraft positioned, as the gate guard, by the Main Guardroom that I did not recognise. Having recently joined the RAF I thought I was well brushed up on my RAF aircraft, but this had me stumped. It looked a bit like a Buccaneer from the front, but it had a delta wing with a high T-tail; it looked fairly modern, as if it should still be flying. I eventually found out that it was a Gloster Javelin, an all-weather interceptor aircraft that served with the RAF in the late 1950s and most of the 1960s. At its height in the early 1960s there were about fifteen squadrons based in the UK and Germany with over 400 Javelins built.

So, with that many aircraft, how did I not know about it, never mind hear about it? That got me thinking about what other aircraft there were that I did not know about. Now don't get me wrong, I'm no plane spotter, nor am I the world's leading expert on strange-looking aircraft, but the realisation that there ARE strange-looking aircraft and that some actually flew was intriguing. I must admit I hold to the view that if a plane is aesthetically pleasing to the eye then it's probably a fantastic one to fly. So if you'd like to find out whether a car, a doughnut or a bedstead can fly, or if it's better for an aircraft to have twelve wings, no wings or a diagonal wing, then read on.

I hope you enjoy this book and marvel, chuckle, shake your head or raise an eyebrow at the wide variety of aircraft that have tried to 'slip the surly bonds of earth', but remember, someone has given blood, sweat and tears to realise their dreams – or not.

RORY UNDERWOOD

I grew up during the 1950s and, like most young boys, was always interested in aircraft. It was an exciting era for young aircraft enthusiasts. We saw the 'last gasp' of the piston-engined airliner, epitomised by the Lockheed Super Constellation and Douglas DC7C with their four mighty Wright Cyclone turbo-compound radial engines spewing flames from the exhausts at full throttle on take-off. Then the age of the jet airliner dawned with the arrival of the Comet, whilst the turboprop quickly became the last nail in the coffin for the piston-engined airliner.

On the military side there was the Hawker Hunter, the Supermarine Swift, the DH110 and the American Super Sabre amongst many others. Perhaps most exciting to me at that time was the English Electric P1, which in turn would evolve into the Lightning. Fearsome looking, in its P1B form it was so powerful with its twin Rolls-Royce Avon jets with afterburners that it could accelerate in a vertical climb – the first aircraft ever to be able to achieve this. I had never seen anything like it before.

These were the 'normal' aircraft of my youth. If I had been asked at the time to name a 'strange' aircraft, I suppose I might have mentioned the de Havilland Dragon Rapide, an oddball biplane still flying commercially, and maybe the Bristol Freighter, which opened its enormous nose to swallow cars, around four or six at a time, to fly them across the

Channel. That was about all I knew about 'strange' aircraft back then.

It was only in my later years that I came to realise that really strange, oddball aircraft have been around since the very beginnings of aviation. These have included:

- An aircraft with 200 separate wings.
- A fully inflatable aircraft.
- A giant plane that flew at 500kph at an altitude of just 4m above the water.
- A completely round aeroplane.
- An aircraft that flaps its wings just like a bird.
- Totally asymmetrical aircraft.
- Aircraft that were nothing more than flying bombs with a pilot strapped inside with no means of ever landing.

My eyes were opened, and so this book came into being. Classifying aircraft as 'strange' is in no way a judgment on them. Some truly strange aircraft were exceptionally good in every way, whilst others were unadulterated crap. But, good or bad, the criterion for inclusion here is that, in one way or another, the aircraft was indeed really 'strange'.

But what precisely does the word 'strange' mean? Looking at an online dictionary I found that 'strange' is defined as 'an adjective meaning unusual or surprising; difficult to understand or explain'. The dictionary also, helpfully, provided a list of synonyms for 'strange'. These included: unusual, odd, curious, peculiar, funny, bizarre, weird, uncanny, queer, unexpected, unfamiliar, abnormal, atypical, anomalous, untypical, different, out of the ordinary, out of the way, extraordinary, remarkable, puzzling, mystifying, mysterious, perplexing, baffling, unaccountable, inexplicable, incongruous, uncommon, irregular, singular, deviant, aberrant, freak, freakish, surreal.

Having finished writing the book, I looked back at these synonyms and realised that quite a large number of the aircraft covered manage the amazing feat of qualifying under nearly all the headings at the same time – some achievement by the aeronautical designers and engineers. This book is intended as a lasting monument to those designers and engineers.

A HEALTH WARNING

The author and publisher would like to point out that some of the content of this book is quite potent, showing what aircraft designers are capable of doing if not kept under careful control, and that this might put some readers off air travel so severely that even the sound of an aircraft, or the sight of an airline ticket, might induce instant death. The author and publisher can accept no responsibility for such a demise but would be most interested to hear about any such event as it would make the second book in the series that much more entertaining.

For the purposes of this book, the 'strange aircraft' have been classified under fourteen different headings:

- Simply awesome.
- Planes perfectly designed to kill the people flying them.
- Divine intervention or magic mushrooms?
- Don't let aircraft designers go for a pub lunch.
- Plane bonkers.
- Designers with latent wing fetishes.
- Is double vision a common problem in the aeronautical design office?
- Aircraft designed by a kiddies' origami class.
- What happens when aircraft designers wear the wrong spectacles.
- Is it a car? Is it a plane?
- Some designers just forget things.
- Vertical take-off oddities.
- Strange goings-on on the water.
- Is it a frisbee? Is it a boomerang?

This is of course an extremely scientific classification, worked on at considerable intellectual altitude for a whole evening whilst seeking inspiration from a couple of bottles of rather splendid Chateau Gatwick North Terminal '69.

On sober reflection the following morning, after a rough landing, it became evident that a mere two categories – Plain bonkers and Simply awesome – might have covered 90 per cent plus of all the strange aircraft. But being very ecologically minded, and so not wishing to waste the sheet of paper I'd scribbled the ideas on the evening before, I decided to stick with the fourteen categories.

A WEALTH WARNING

Upon reading this book, some readers may decide that air travel is simply too dangerous to contemplate under any circumstances, not because passenger aircraft are intrinsically unsafe today, but because there may be a small chance of your flight encountering one or other of the strange planes described here at 30,000ft.

The reader may then feel compelled to complete all journeys by land or sea, using of course luxury liners at vast expense. The author and publisher accept no responsibility for bankruptcy, divorce or insanity thereby triggered by the exposure to the world of 'strange aircraft'.

Having already published a book on bizarre cars, the author would like to point out that with the eventual completion of the trilogy with a volume on strange ships, virtually all travel, with the exception of walking, may become impossible for many.

Life can be a bitch.

SIMPLY AWESOME

This category is self-explanatory. It is about the really outlandish freaks that have taken to the air, from the Russian Kalinin K-7, which put on a good impersonation of a cross between a flying battleship and a tower block, and the Hughes Hercules or 'Spruce Goose' whose 97m wingspan has never been exceeded, to the vast Vickers Type C, which looked as though it was flying backwards, and the truly awesome (and rather inappropriately named!) Convair B-36 'Peacemaker', which needed six massive piston engines and four jet engines just to get off the ground.

KALININ K-7 FLYING FORTRESS

A CROSS BETWEEN A FLYING BATTLESHIP AND A TOWER BLOCK

I can imagine the mood in the Kalinin drawing office after a long Friday lunch break featuring some rather special 'mushroom' soup and maybe the odd vodka or ten. The big boss thinks to himself: Why do we only use aircraft designers here, when, with a little imagination, we could pull together a new design group consisting of one who has spent a career designing battleships, another who specialised in tanks, one who majored on tower blocks, one without a portfolio but who is certified insane and has a pathological fear of anything sensible, a 12-year-old Lego fanatic, plus one with a slight knowledge of aviation but an IQ below 25. Introduce them to someone who, for some strange reason, has a vast collection of redundant aero engines and a shed load of money, and ask them to build a plane?

What a great mould-breaking idea. What they would come up with might well look like the Kalinin K-7. With its fourteen engines, twelve at the front and two facing backwards, two battleship-type gun turrets, one inverted, accommodation for 120 passengers inside the windowless wings, and a flight deck which did quite a good impersonation of a shopping centre, it was, you might agree, just a tad strange.

So would anyone seriously build a leviathan like this? Of course not. That's not the real K-7, just a 'design exercise'. On the critical day someone went round the design office with cups of 'sensible juice', and they came up with the actual K-7, which of course was a sensible, conservative and conventional design. Well, in truth it wasn't that at all. So what did it look like? That is rather difficult to answer, because just one was built and it crashed on its seventh test flight, only poor-quality photographs surviving. However, an accurate scale model has been built which shows how very 'sensible' the real K-7 was.

The 'sensible' version had just seven Mikulin V12 piston engines, and the battleship turrets had been dropped. However, the design

Kalinin K-7.

Kalinin K-7.

was notable for having five open machine-gun stations manned by unfortunate aircrew who were evidently immune to the 140mph winds when the K-7 was going flat out. It still had accommodation for 120 agoraphobic passengers inside the windowless wings, and was twice as wide as it was long. It wasn't meant to be like that, though. The initial design had much longer tail booms, but the very first flight in 1933 showed extreme instability and serious vibration, the whole plane shaking violently in resonance to the engines. So the boom was shortened, probably the result of guesswork, for it didn't help at all as it turned out. The vibration was so bad that the shortened boom structure shook itself to pieces on the seventh flight, killing all the crew and one on the ground. Two more prototypes had been planned but were never built.

It is thought that sabotage may have been responsible. Fingers have been pointed at the competing design office of Andrei Tupolev, but in any case the Kalinin designs were doomed to failure. Just after the first test flight Pravda announced the K-7 as being 'a victory of utmost political importance' since it had been built from Russian, rather than imported, steel. The rhetoric went rather silent after the crash. So did Konstantin Kalinin … he was executed as an 'enemy of the State' by Stalin in 1938.

Crew	11
Ideal IQ of pilot	<75
Capacity	120 passengers (brave & not claustrophobic)
Length	28m (91ft 10in)
Wingspan	53m (173ft 10in)
Wing area	454m² (7,500 sheets of A4 paper)
Height	12.4m (40ft 8in)
Weight empty	24,400kg (53,680lb)
Weight loaded	38,000kg (83,600lb)
Engines	7 x Mikulin AM-34F V12 piston engines
Power	560kW (750hp) each
Max speed	225kph
Service ceiling	4,000m

HUGHES H-4 HERCULES
A GREAT POTENTIAL SOURCE OF BARBEQUE FUEL

In terms of strangeness, the Hughes H-4 Hercules, commonly called the 'Spruce Goose', actually looks fairly normal. It's got wings, two of them, one each side, it has a tail, at the back, and carries its eight engines in the conventional position. OK, it's large, very large ... well extremely large in fact. Actually in terms of wingspan (97.54m) it is still the largest aircraft ever built. The largest ever aircraft in terms of weight, the Antonov An-225 Mriya, makes do with tiny wings of only 88m span. I suppose that alone is sufficient to elevate the Hercules into the world of bizarreness, but there is more:

- It was commissioned in 1942 to be a military transport, to carry equipment across the Atlantic for the war effort. Unfortunately it took so long to build that by 1947, when it was ready, the war had already been over for two years, and the H-4 had been rather forgotten about.
- It was built entirely of wood, mainly plywood laminates, so probably could have been knocked together by a furniture company for a fraction of the cost and in half the time. Indeed the wooden de Havilland Mosquito was built by furniture companies like Ercol in High Wycombe.

- In spite of its nickname, which Howard Hughes hated, it didn't contain one single ounce of spruce at all. The wood was all birch.
- It cost $25 million to build, and that's in 1940 dollars. That translates into $38.6 billion in today's money, which makes the latest $2.4 billion American B2 Spirit stealth bomber look like a cheap line from Poundland.
- It only ever flew once, a journey of just 1.6km in 1947. The photograph was taken just before it became airborne at the hands of Howard Hughes himself.
- That makes it the most expensive journey of all time. In terms of production costs alone that amounts to $26 billion per kilometre in 2014 money, even more than First Great Western's peak rail fare from Maidenhead to London Paddington.
- It never reached an altitude of more than 20m, so in effect throughout its life it was a ground effect aircraft like the Caspian Sea Monster.

Hughes H-4 Hercules.

- After its only flight it was carefully maintained by a full-time ground crew of 300. This was reduced to a 'skeleton' staff of just fifty in 1962, but on Hughes' death in 1976 the team was disbanded.
- The hangar where it was built was more recently used to film some scenes for the film *Titanic*, which somehow seems appropriate although I cannot for the life of me think why it should.

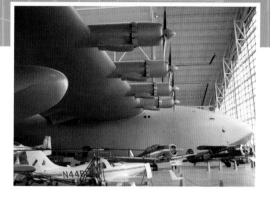

Spruce Goose 2.

Crew	3
Length	66.65m (218ft 8in)
Wingspan	97.54m (320ft 0in)
Height	24.18m (79ft 3in)
Weight loaded	180,000kg (396,000lb)
Barbecue equivalents	200,000
Engines	8 x Pratt & Whitney R-4360 Wasp Major radials
Power	2,640kW (3,540hp) each
Propellers	four-blade Hamilton Standard 5.23m diameter
Cruising speed	408kph
Max range	4,800km
Actual range	1.5km
Service ceiling	6,370m
Actual ceiling	20m

The second photograph shows the H-4 in its current home at the Evergreen Aviation Museum in Oregon, where its staggering size is evident. It looks as though it might eat those small aircraft for breakfast.

In spite of its staggeringly high cost, there is one small crumb of comfort about the H-4. Unlike most aircraft, if the worst came to the worst, and the cost of its preservation became too much, it could be turned into charcoal and used to fuel nearly 200,000 barbecues.

ANTANOV AN-225 MRIYA

QUITE SIMPLY THE WORLD'S LARGEST AIRCRAFT

Strange is almost certainly the wrong word to describe the An-225. Unusual, yes. Awesome, yes. The An-225 is quite simply the largest aircraft in the world, and in terms of lifting power the biggest of all time.

The An-225 was originally developed from the An-124 specifically to carry the Buran space plane,

the Russian version of the space shuttle. The photograph shows it performing this role. Built in 1988, it is still in commercial operation with Antonov Airlines carrying outsize loads.

The An-225 holds the world record for the heaviest single item (a gas power plant weighing 189,980kg),

the heaviest total load (253,820kg) and the longest payload (42m wind turbine blades) in history.

A second An-225 was due for completion in 2008, but the work fell behind and was abandoned. In 2011 Antonov announced that a second and larger An-225, with a lifting capacity of 250 tons, was being built and could be completed by 2014. No further official announcements have been made, although some sources say it is 60–70 per cent completed.

Crew	6
Length	84.0m (275ft 7in)
Wingspan	88.4m (290ft 0in)
Height	18.1m (59ft 4in)
Weight empty	285,000kg (627,000lb)
Weight loaded	640,000kg (1,408,000lb)
Engines	6 x ZMKB Progress D-18 turbofans
Power	229.5kN (51,600lbf) thrust each
Cruising speed	800kph
Max speed	850kph
Max range	15,400km
Service ceiling	11,000m
Number built	1

Antonov An-225.

BOEING DREAMLIFTER

A BOEING 747 ON STEROIDS

The Boeing Dreamlifter was built for one very specialised task, that of moving components for the Dreamliner between Japan and Italy to the United States. In total four were built, all being conversions of old 747s. The first 4 or 5m of the fuselage look just like the 747 donor plane, but thereafter the fuselage looks like a steroid fuelled design aberration.

The first conversion remained in the unusual colour scheme shown in the photograph for some time, emphasising the outlandish nature of the beast. It looked rather like a 747 wearing a very thick overcoat. It is said that Scott Carson, the president of Boeing Commercial Airplanes, jokingly apologised to 747 designer Joe Sutter, saying 'sorry for what we did to your plane'.

However, the Dreamlifter is very special. It has the largest cargo hold of any plane ever built, with a capacity of 1,840m³, three times the size of the hold on a 747-400F freighter. The tail swings open, and the Dreamlifter is loaded using the world's longest cargo loader.

Crew	2
Length	71.68m (235ft 2in)
Wingspan	64.4m (211ft 3in)
Height	21.54m (70ft 8in)
Weight empty	180,530kg (397,166lb)
Weight loaded	364,235kg (801,317lb)
Engines	4 x Pratt & Whitney 4062
Power	282kN (63,300lbf) thrust each
Cruising speed	878kph
Number built	4

Boeing Dreamlifter.

AIRBUS BELUGA

IS THIS THE UGLIEST AIRCRAFT OF ALL TIME?

If any aircraft were capable of inducing bad dreams, it must surely be the hunchback Beluga. It's a good candidate for the ugliest aircraft of all time.

The Beluga is a version of the standard Airbus A300-600 wide-body airliner but modified to carry oversized cargoes, and in particular aircraft parts. It was originally called the Super Transporter, but the name Beluga quickly caught on.

The Airbus programme required aircraft parts to be made in four different countries: the UK, France, Germany and Spain. Each country makes entire sections of the aircraft, and these need to be transported to the place where the jigsaw is finally put together. Generally speaking, the wings and landing gear are made in the UK, the tail and doors in Spain, the fuselage in Germany, and the nose and centre section in France. Final assembly is in Toulouse, Hamburg or Seville.

Construction of the Beluga began in 1992, with the first flight in 1994. After 335 hours of test flying, certification was awarded in October 1995. Eventually five were built, and all remain in active service. Perhaps the Beluga's strangest cargo was a painting; the picture 'Liberty Leading the People', by Delacroix, which had hung in the Louvre since 1874, was flown from Paris to Tokyo in a vertical position inside a special pressurised and isothermal container. The painting measures 2.99m by 3.62m, too large for a 747.

Airbus Beluga.

Crew	2
Length	56.2m (184ft 2in)
Wingspan	44.84m (147ft 1in)
Height	17.24m (56ft 6in)
Weight empty	86,000kg (189,200lb)
Weight loaded	155,000kg (341,000lb)
Engines	2 x General Electric CF6-80C2A8
Range	2,779km (40t load) 4,632km (26t load)
Number built	5

BOEING B-377 SG SUPER GUPPY

A CLASSIC EXAMPLE OF AERONAUTIC RECYCLING

The Aero Spacelines 'Super Guppy' was originally developed in the 1960s for the NASA programme to transport sections of shuttles and rockets. Although it looked quite futuristic, it was in fact a modified 1940s Boeing 377 Stratocruiser, equipped with Pratt & Whitney turboprops to replace the piston engines. The fuselage was lengthened to 43m and the top part ballooned out to a maximum diameter of 7.6m.

Later versions of the Super Guppy (which became its official name) only used part of the Stratocruiser fuselage, the rest coming from Boeing's 'parts bin'. The nose gear, for example, was Boeing 707 but rotated by 180°.

The Super Guppy was used in the 1970s in the early days of the Airbus programme in Europe to move aircraft sections from country to country. By the 1970s the Stratocruiser was already 30-plus years old, but this didn't stop Airbus buying the right to build the aircraft, and two more were constructed in 1982 and 1983, by which time the basic design was 40 years old.

By the early 1990s the Super Guppy was showing its age, and its carrying capacity had started to look limited compared to the C5 Galaxy and Antanov 124. The need for more carrying capacity spawned the development of the Beluga, an aircraft that achieved the almost impossible task of being even uglier than the Super Guppy.

B-377 SG Super Guppy. (Wikimedia Commons courtesy of aeroprints.com)

Crew	2
Length	43.84m (143ft 10in)
Wingspan	47.63m (156ft 3in)
Height	14.78m (48ft 6in)
Weight empty	46,039kg (94,686lb)
Weight loaded	77,110kg (169,642lb)
Engines	4 x Allison 501-D22C turboprops
Power	3,491kW (4,680hp) each
Max speed	463kph
Range	3,219km
Ceiling	7,620m
Number built	5 (1 SG + 4 SGT with updated design)

SAUNDERS ROE PRINCESS

THE LARGEST ALL-METAL FLYING BOAT EVER BUILT

In 1945 the Ministry of Supply asked Saunders Roe to bid for the contract to build a long-range flying boat for BOAC. The plan was to use them on the transatlantic route.

The Princess was unusual in a number of ways. Firstly it had ten engines but, at first sight, only six propellers. In fact the inner sets of propellers were pairs of contra-rotating props, each driven by a separate engine.

Secondly, the vast plane was designed to carry just 105 passengers, but in unparalleled luxury, and it would almost certainly never have been economic to operate across the Atlantic.

Thirdly, and strangest of all, there was a serious plan in 1958 to convert the three Princesses built to nuclear power. However, the plan came to nothing, perhaps very fortunately.

There was a sad end to the Princess. After three had been built it soon became apparent that there would be no need for them. Transatlantic flight was changing in the 1950s and large powerful land-planes, like the DC-7C and Super Constellation, were dominating the route, and were much more economical both to build and to operate. The three Princess flying boats were mothballed, whilst many different plans to reuse them came and went. Finally, in 1964, a plan was put forward to use them for transporting sections of Saturn V rockets for NASA. The plan looked feasible, but when the three aircraft were finally removed from storage it was found that they had corroded so badly they were no longer airworthy. They were all broken up in 1967. It was a sad end for a mighty aircraft.

Crew	6 (2 pilots, 2 flight engineers, radio operator & navigator)
Length	45m (147ft 7in)
Wingspan	66.9m (219ft 6in)
Height	16.99m (55ft 9in)
Weight empty	86,183kg (189,603lb)
Weight loaded	149,685kg (329,300lb)
Engines	8 x Bristol Proteus 610 turboprops
	2 x Bristol Proteus 600 turboprops
Power	1,528kW (2,050hp) each (Proteus 610 & 600)
Max speed	611kph
Range	9,205km
Ceiling	11,887m
Number built	3

Saunders Roe SR45 Princess.

TUPOLEV TU-95 BEAR

WHEN IT TURNS 100 WILL IT GET A TELEGRAM FROM THE PRESIDENT OF RUSSIA?

The Tu-95 'Bear' is as awesome as it is strange. It first flew in 1952, and is expected to remain in active service until at least 2040, by which time it will be 88 years old. Give it a few more years and it will become a centenarian! An eighty-eight-year active service life on its own qualifies the Bear as strange and unique.

But the strangeness goes beyond mere longevity:

Tupolev Tu-95 Bear.
(Wikimedia Commons courtesy RAF MOD)

Crew	6–7
Length	46.2m (151ft 7in)
Wingspan	50.1m (164ft 4in)
Height	12.12m (39ft 9in)
Weight empty	90,000kg (198,000lb)
Weight loaded	171,0000kg (376,200lb)
Engines	4 x Kuznetsov NK-12M turboprops
Power	11,000kW (14,800shp) each
Max speed	920kph
Max range	15,000km
Service ceiling	13,716m
Armament	2 x 23mm cannon plus 15,000kg of missiles

- It is the only turboprop powered strategic bomber in operational use.
- Equally it is the only propeller-driven strategic bomber.
- It has wings sharply swept back at 35°.
- A civilian version, the Tu114, holds the record as the world's fastest propeller-driven aircraft, achieving 540mph.
- A Tu-95 carried and dropped the nuclear AN602 Tsar Bomba, the largest and most powerful bomb ever detonated.
- Each of the four engines drives two propellers, contra-rotating.
- The propellers are the largest ever seen on a production aircraft. Their size necessitates the very tall undercarriage.
- The tips of the propeller blades travel at supersonic speed, resulting in the Tu-95 being the noisiest aircraft ever to fly. So noisy are the Bears that they have been detected by US underwater sonars thousands of miles away in the Atlantic.
- It has an unprecedented range for a heavy bomber of over 8,000 miles.

BRISTOL BRABAZON

PROBABLY THE MOST LUXURIOUS AIRLINER EVER BUILT

The Bristol Brabazon was almost unbelievably luxurious. It was conceived in 1943 by the Brabazon Committee, which had been set up to plan how the UK should return to civil aircraft production when the war was over. The committee recommended the construction of four of the five designs they had studied. Type 1 was a very large transatlantic airliner, Type 2 short haul, Type 3 a medium-range airliner for multiple-stage Empire routes and Type 4 a jet-powered airliner (which would become the Comet).

The Type 1 became the Brabazon. The technical specification was awesome enough. A length of 54m, a wingspan of 70.1m (11m greater than a 747) and eight engines grouped in pairs, driving contra-rotating propellers.

But what made the Brabazon truly strange, and quite amazing, was the passenger accommodation. The Committee had assumed the very wealthy people travelling across the Atlantic would see a long air journey as tedious and uncomfortable. To make the journey more comfortable for this elite group the plane was designed to carry just 100 passengers, less than one quarter of similarly sized modern airliners.

Each passenger had 6m^2 of space, about the size of a small car, and the plane also had eighty sleeping berths, a dining room, a thirty-seven-seat cinema, a promenade and a bar. To accommodate all this luxury the Brabazon had an 8m-diameter

Crew	6–12
Passengers	100
Length	54.0m (177ft 2in)
Wingspan	70m (229ft 8in)
Height	15.0m (49ft 3in)
Weight empty	65,820kg (165,429lb)
Weight loaded	130,000kg (286,000lb)
Engines	8 x Bristol Centaurus radial engine
Power	1,860kW (2,650hp) each
Propellers	8 x 4.9m, three wooden blades
Cruising speed	400kph
Max speed	480kph
Max range	8,900km
Service ceiling	7,600m

Bristol Brabazon.

fuselage, which is 1.5m greater than a Boeing 747.

The only prototype was first flown in 1949, just in time for the government to decide it was too large and expensive to be of any practical use. It was broken up for scrap in 1953 along with the uncompleted turboprop Brabazon Mk II.

Photographs of the actual prototype Brabazon are relatively few and the quality is not good. The photograph shown here is of a model. However, seeing this model alongside some contemporary aircraft helps to emphasise its enormous size.

VICKERS TYPE C

COULD THIS BOMBER SIMPLY SCARE THE ENEMY TO DEATH?

The Vickers Type C was one of a number of designs produced in response to an RAF brief for a 'super bomber', with a long range, adequate defensive armament and a very large bomb load. The intention was for it to carry, amongst others, Barnes Wallis' 10,000kg 'earthquake bomb', also known as the Grand Slam bomb. Several companies produced designs, amongst whom Vickers produced a sequence of designs (A, B, C etc.) of which the Type C was the strangest.

One feature of the Type C, with its main wings set back near the tail, and a pair of small canard wings at the front, is that from the ground it would have appeared to be flying backwards. This alone might have been sufficient to scare those on the ground to death, without the expense of actually dropping bombs.

However, when it became apparent that it would take at least five years to design, build and test the 'super bomber' the project was cancelled. The practical success of the Lancaster was another nail in the coffin.

Crew	?
Length	29m (95ft 2in)
Wingspan	64m (210ft 0in)
Weight loaded	80,741kg (177,630lb)
Engines	6 x Bristol Centaurus with superchargers
Power	2,192kW (2,940hp) each
Max speed	621kph
Ceiling	10,600m
Armament	25 x 400kg bombs
	5 x 20mm + 2 x 0.5in guns

Vickers Type C. (Courtesy of Martin Letts at www.xplanes3d.com)

CONVAIR B-36 PEACEMAKER
WAS THIS THE MOST AWESOME BOMBER EVER BUILT?

Let's look at the facts first. The Convair B-36 'Peacemaker':

- Was the largest serial production piston engine aircraft ever made.
- Had the longest wingspan of any combat aircraft ever built, even to this day.
- Was the first aircraft capable of dropping the atomic bomb.
- Was the first manned bomber with an unrefuelled intercontinental range, being able to remain airborne for over forty hours.
- Uniquely combined four jet engines with six massive piston engines, each with 28 cylinders.
- Was too large for any maintenance hangars, and had to be serviced out in the open. A change of spark plugs involved 336 units.
- Had wings that were thick enough to allow the flight engineer to access the engines and landing gear from inside.
- Had six massive piston engines that consumed a total of around 600 gallons (2,280 litres) of engine oil per flight.

Apart from all that, the Peacemaker was just a simple, ordinary, run-of-the-mill bomber.

The origin of the Peacemaker goes back to 1941, when there was a real fear that Britain would fall to Nazi Germany. In that event bombing missions against Hitler could not be based in Europe, and there would be a need for extremely long-range bombing missions from North America. The bomber would

Convair B-36 Peacemaker.

need a range of 9,200km (5,700 miles), the distance from Gander in Newfoundland to Berlin and back. The US government opened a design competition for a bomber with a range of 19,000km (12,000 miles), a service ceiling of 14,000m (45,000ft) and a top speed of 720kph (450mph). The specification was too much for the day, and was significantly reduced.

But as the Japanese conflict escalated the need again arose for a super-long-range bomber, and development work started on the B-36. But the aircraft was not unveiled until August 1945, and flew for the first time in August 1946. So, although too late for the Second World War, it was well placed to face the Soviet threat in the Cold War.

In reality the B-36 was obsolete before it ever took off, being piston engined in what had become a jet age. But its range and lifting power remained useful in the early nuclear age, even though it proved very unreliable and extremely expensive to operate. The scrapping of the B-36s started in 1956, and the last one was withdrawn from operation in 1959.

Crew	13
Length	49.42m (230ft 0in)
Wingspan	70.12m (230ft 0in)
Height	14.25m (46ft 9in)
Weight empty	75,530kg (166,165lb)
Weight loaded	119,318kg (262,500lb)
Engines	6 x Pratt & Whitney R-4360-53 Wasp Major radial
	4 x General Electric J47 turbojets
Power	2,835kW (3,800hp) Wasp Majors each
	23.2kN (5,200lbf) GE turbojets each
Max speed	672kph (418mph)
Range	16,000km (10,000 miles)
Ceiling	13,300m (43,600ft)
Armament	2 x 20mm M24A1 autocannons in rear turret
	39,000kg (86,000lb) bombs

PLANES PERFECTLY DESIGNED TO KILL THE PEOPLE FLYING THEM

The second section of this book is devoted to aircraft designed, on the face of it, with the main intention of killing those who flew them. Many achieved this objective with spectacular, and in some cases total, success.

In most cases it is not clear whether the fatal design was the product of a sinister secret society of sadistic aircraft designers who hated pilots, crew and passengers alike, or simply one of utter incompetence and an all-pervasive lack of understanding about what keeps heavy lumps of metal up in the air.

For obvious reasons most of these aircraft no longer exist as they largely did succeed in killing those who flew them. As a result many of the photographs are quite old and not of very high quality.

HEINKEL HE-162 VOLKSJAGER

If you were to assemble a team of Nobel Prize-winning scientists, a number of the world's top engineers, and a handful of certified sadistic lunatics, and challenge them under threat of death to design an aircraft guaranteed to kill the pilot, they'd be hard pressed to better the He-162 Volksjager, or 'people's fighter'. This was a product of Germany's increasingly desperate Emergency Fighter Programme in 1945. It was designed to be as cheap and quick to build as possible, and was in effect a disposable aircraft. However, in spite of its crudeness, in 1945 it was the fastest aircraft in the world, at least for the very short time it managed to remain airborne in one piece.

Let's examine the facts:

- The whole development programme, from first madcap idea through first madcap test flight to first madcap crash, was trimmed to just ninety days.
- It was built largely of wood and string, glued together with adhesives that apparently were so acidic they ate into the very wood they were meant to be holding together.

- On the first two test flights, the acidic glue failed and the flying orange box crashed. Maybe disposable pilots were also part of the programme.
- It was designed to be built by unskilled labourers, all skilled labourers by 1945 being either dead or fighting. This must have been less than comforting for the pilot,

Heinkel He-162 Volksjager.

Crew	1
Length	9.05m (29ft 8in)
Wingspan	7.2m (23ft 7in)
Height	2.6m (8ft 6in)
Weight empty	1,660kg (3,652lb)
Weight loaded	2,800kg (6,160lb)
Engine	1 x BMW 003E-1 or E-2 axial flow turbojet
Power	7.85kN (1,765lbf)
Max speed	790kph
Range	975km
Altitude	12,000m
Armament	2 x 20mm MG151/20 autocannons

knowing the 1,700lb of thrust was rapidly propelling him towards his maker in a crudely assembled pile of junk.

- It was designed to be flown by untrained Hitler Youth members.
- If damaged it was meant to be thrown away, like an empty crisp packet or used condom.
- The controls were apparently so complicated that even trained pilots struggled to master the thing, so sticking untrained Hitler Youth in the pilot's seat must have been on a par with recruiting Concorde pilots from the local toddlers' group.
- Some bright spark in the design office thought the logical place for the jet engine was just above and just behind the cockpit cover. So if the pilot had tried to eject, he'd have been sucked into the jet-powered meat mincer and spewed out at the back. Actually, covering the windshield of following Allied Spitfires with blood and minced guts might have been its trump card.
- They gave it a range of just thirty minutes, fifteen minutes out and fifteen back (or, more likely, thirty minutes out and no 'back'). This was good if you wanted to bomb your own airfield but not much use against an enemy, unless he obligingly sat at the end of your runway.
- Finally nobody could agree on what to call this aerial abortion. The government called it Volksjager (people's fighter), the Luftwaffe called it Salamander and the builder Heinkel called it Spatz (sparrow). I think Haufen Scheisse (pile of shit) might have been more appropriate.

So was the flying junk heap a success? No, judging by the figures. During its first month of operation, April 1945, a total of thirteen were lost. However, just two were the result of enemy attack, the rest just spontaneously fell to pieces in the air. Today it might be seen as quite environmentally friendly, in that it never lasted long enough to pollute the air, and it was almost instantly biodegradable.

ROYAL AIRCRAFT FACTORY BE9 'PULPIT'

THE PERFECT AIRCRAFT FOR THE PILOT WHO HATES HIS GUNNER

They say that if you gave 10,000 monkeys typewriters and left them typing for a few thousand years, they'd eventually rewrite the complete works of Shakespeare. However, if you set them a more challenging task, that of thinking of a more stupid location for a gunner on an aircraft than that on the BE9 'Pulpit', I think they'd fail.

During the First World War the British wanted a fighter plane with guns that could shoot forwards. But there was a problem providing such guns on a single-engined aircraft.

Normally, pre-First World War, the gunner would sit behind the pilot and fire either backwards or sideways. Back in 1914 the technology for synchronising a gun and the propeller hadn't been invented, and if the gunner fired forwards, which is the preferred direction when pursuing an enemy, he shot the propeller to pieces, with less than desirable results. One solution was to use a pusher propeller, but the Royal Aircraft Factory (forerunner of the Royal Aircraft Establishment) preferred to use a 'tractor' propeller,

which gave better performance, and so needed a novel new design. This came in the shape of the BE9.

Their simple solution was to attach a small flimsy wooden box just in front of the propeller, and strap the gunner inside it. This became known as the 'pulpit', perhaps to remind the poor gunner that he was likely to meet his maker sooner rather than later. No doubt the gunner was strapped in because, once he realised how horrific his imminent fate would be, he might try to escape. This design did have one or two drawbacks, however:

Royal Aircraft Factory BE9 Pulpit.

- In even the lightest of crashes the gunner would take the full impact and become a sort of human airbag/crumple zone.
- However there was almost certainly a greater risk of the gunner being sucked backwards by the propeller and turned into fine minced meat.
- There was no shielding at all between the gunner and the propeller, so should for example his scarf become loose in the 100mph draught, or should he swing his arm whilst firing the gun, he was in danger of having his head or arms ripped off.
- The gunner simply had no choice but to cling on for dear life until the plane landed or he became too tired. There was no way for the gunner to tell the pilot he was feeling the strain, or would rather go to the pub for a quiet pint, because of the deafening noise from the engine between them. The first the pilot would know about the gunner being tired was when his goggles became covered by the gunner's minced up guts.

It was not a success, and just one was built. Soon the need to place the gunner in such a dangerous position was made unnecessary by the invention of the interrupter gear, which synchronised the gun with the propeller.

Crew	2 (on a good day)
Length	8.84m (29ft 0in)
Wingspan	12.46m (40ft 11in)
Height	3.48m (11ft 5in)
Engine	1 x RAF 1a V-8
Power	67kW (90hp)
Max speed	131kph (82mph)
Climb rate	305m in 4.5 minutes
Armament	1 x Lewis gun

MITSUBISHI G4M 'BETTY'

THE FLYING ZIPPO LIGHTER

A Zippo lighter is a handy little device, full of petrol, which produces a nice small flame in the presence of a tiny spark. The Mitsubishi G4M 'Betty' was a bloody enormous device, full of petrol, which produced a ******* gigantic flame in the presence of a tiny spark. Therein lay the problem.

The G4M was designed to be a quick, light and ridiculously long-range bomber. Its range was around 3,000 miles, quite unnecessary for Japan, which actually didn't have many targets to bomb anyway, and those that it did have were virtually on their doorstep. In order to gain this impressive but totally unnecessary range, it was equipped with enormous fuel tanks, but it also had many rather necessary bits stripped off to reduce weight. So there was no armour covering the fuel tanks, the tanks themselves were basically simple oil drums with no self-sealing coating, and so the whole plane was basically a long fragile petrol tank with a cockpit and two engines rather self-consciously bolted on the front.

The American army air forces, who mostly faced the 'Betty', quickly realised that one single shot from even a tiny-calibre gun would reduce the G4M into an infernal fireball. It became known as the 'One Shot Lighter'.

Crew	7 (with a death wish)
Length	24.9m (81ft 8in)
Wingspan	24.9m (81ft 8in)
Height	4.9m (16ft 1in)
Weight empty	6,741kg (14,830lb)
Weight loaded	9,500kg (20,900lb)
Engines	2 x Mitsubishi MK4A-11 14-cylinder radials
Power	1,141kW (1,530hp) each
Max speed	428kph
Range	5,040km each way (max)
Altitude	8,500m (subject to not exploding)
Armament	1 x Type 99 20mm cannon
	4 x 7.7mm Type 92 machine guns
	1 x 858kg Type 91 aerial torpedo or
	1 x 800kg bomb or
	4 x 250kg bombs

Mitsubishi G4M Betty.

It was designed to be quick, light and long range. Well, to some extent it succeeded; it was 'quick' in the sense that it quickly exploded, it was 'light' in the sense that the resulting fireball would light up the surroundings, and long range in the sense, I suppose, that the unfortunate crew would end up a long, long way from home ... somewhere like heaven, or more likely hell.

Maybe the Mitsubishi G4M 'Betty' missed its true vocation, as a bonfire night spectacular. One simple spark and the whole bonfire night sky would have been transformed into a technicolour wonderland ... not so sure about the fate of the pilot, though.

For some reason the G4M was never very popular with aircrews!

The photograph shows a 'Betty' that was captured in 1945. Oh, and one last important point ... I've never managed to find out why it was nicknamed 'Betty'.

BACHEM BA-349 NATTER

BACHEM NUTTER, OR FLYING COFFIN, WOULD HAVE BEEN BETTER NAMES

By March 1945 the Germans were becoming desperate, recognising that the war was all but lost. They had already developed the V1 and V2 'vengeance' weapons, and decided to go one step further with a manned version. Faced with a shortage of airfields, and a dire shortage of materials, they reasoned that a rocket-powered plane, launched vertically, with a flimsy disposable body, was the answer. So came about the Bachem BA-349 Natter.

The idea was that the Natter would be launched vertically, shoot down the enemy planes, and then eject both the pilot and the rocket engine whilst the flimsy fuselage simply fell to Earth. The Germans reasoned that as there was no normal take-off and no landing at all, no skill was involved so it could be 'flown' by 'pilots' with no flying experience at all. Seems quite logical.

So, what could possibly be wrong with this ingenious design? Consider the facts:

- It was built of wood and glued together, and not very well.
- The wingspan was a mere 4m so if the engine cut out, or just fell off, it would glide gently to the ground in the same way a washing machine might, for example.

- It had rockets capable of producing a massive 4,000lb of thrust – quite a lot for a plane, a massive overkill for a flimsy wooden box.
- It was fired vertically upwards at speeds of up to 500mph.

Crew	1 (desirable IQ <60)
Length	6m (19ft 8in)
Wingspan	4m (13ft 2in)
Height	2.25m (7ft 5in)
Wing area	4.7m²
Weight empty	880kg (1,936lb)
Gross weight	2,232kg (4,910lb)
Engines	1 x Walter HWK 109-509C-1 rocket
	4 x Schmidding SG34 solid-fuel boosters
Cruising speed	800kph (497mph)
Max speed	1,000kph (621mph)
Range	40km
Endurance	4.4 minutes
Service ceiling	12,000m (39,370ft)
Armament	24 Henschel Hs 297 Fohn rocket shells

- It was 'piloted' by people with no flying experience whatsoever.
- It was equipped with thirty-six unguided rockets, which, if fired too close together, could rip the wooden box apart.
- It was not designed to land, and had no ejector seat. So the unfortunate 'pilot' had to unbuckle himself and leap out at around 600mph having opened a canopy held on by old furniture hinges. The likelihood is that he'd have been sliced in two by the 600mph tail, anyway.
- On the first test flight the canopy blew off hitting the 'pilot' on the head and sending the plane into a nosedive and crash.
- Its range was a 'massive' 40km, just enough to lose sight of the launch pad.
- Total endurance was around four minutes, very brief but certainly long enough to produce a soiled flying suit.

Even the Germans quickly realised it was a daft idea, but not before they'd built a further thirty-six … they must have said 'Oh Mein Gott' very slowly. Before the war ended they destroyed the remaining ones that hadn't destroyed themselves, as they feared the Allies might steal their 'ingenious' idea. However, why anyone should want to steal the design of a plane that killed more of its own pilots than the enemy's is a complete mystery. Or maybe they just feared becoming a laughing stock.

Maybe it should have been called the Nutter rather than the Natter, in recognition of the designer's evident intellectual skills.

Bachem BA-349 Natter.

FIESELER FI 103R-IV REICHENBERG

A PLANE THAT GOES LIKE A BOMB … LITERALLY

The logic was simple. The V1 flying bomb was not very accurate, and fell to earth and exploded once the fuel to the engine was cut off after a predetermined time. So, why not strap a pilot to the flying bomb so he could steer it more accurately to its target. Simple. It was perhaps the clearest indication in the whole war that Germany hated its own pilots.

The designers took the basic V1 design, hollowed out a tiny 'cockpit' just in front of the pulse jet, and fitted it with a simple plywood seat. It was launched from a larger aircraft, upon which the pilot would then steer the thing towards the intended target, presumably baling out at the last minute.

The minor technical flaw here is that the pilot's head was about 12in ahead of the pulse jet input, and about 6in below it. So, upon ejecting, he would have been immediately sucked into the pulsejet and turned into cooked mince meat.

So dangerous was the Fieseler FI 103R-IV Reichenburg seen to be that

Crew	1 (preferably with a death wish)
Length	8m (26ft 3in)
Wingspan	5.7m(18ft 8in)
Weight loaded	2,250kg (4,950lb)
Engine	1 x Argus As014 pulse jet
Cruising speed	650kph
Max speed	800kph
Range	330km
Armament	the whole thing was a bomb

Fieseler Reichenberg. (Wikimedia Commons courtesy of Chriusha)

the 'volunteer' pilots were required to sign contracts stating they understood it was suicide. The official estimate was that less than 1 per cent of pilots were expected to survive. Not a sound career move for a professional pilot. Pictures are rare (for obvious reasons) and not of the best quality.

By October 1944 the Japanese were becoming increasingly desperate in their fight against the Allied warships in the Pacific, and in particular feared an invasion of Japan, which of course never happened. And so began the kamikaze suicide missions.

At first a variety of existing fighter planes was used, each stuffed full of explosives. However, the existing aircraft had one distinct disadvantage for this role. In the interests of the return journey from a mission, aircraft had things like landing gear, removable cockpit hatches, lots of instruments etc., which added weight and occupied space that could be taken up with explosives. But as there was never any intention that the planes would return, most of the extra equipment was unnecessary.

The solution was to design a plane specifically for a one-way flight. I think that alone warrants inclusion here as strange.

The Nakajima Ki-115 was a custom built 'one-way' aircraft. Amongst the features were:

Crew	1
Length	8.55m (28ft 1in)
Wingspan	8.60m (28ft 3in)
Height	3.3m (10ft 10in)
Weight empty	1,640kg (3,608lb)
Weight loaded	2,580kg (5,676lb)
Engines	1 x Nakajima Ha-35 Type 23 radial engine
	2 x rocket accelerators (later versions)
Power	860kW (1,150hp)
Max speed	550kph
Range	1,200km
Altitude	12,000m
Armament	1 x 250kg or 1 x 500kg or 1 x 800kg bomb

- It didn't have landing gear, as it would never land. Instead it had 'take-off' gear, which was jettisoned immediately after take-off for reuse.
- Apparently this gave a very rough ride for take-off, so shock absorbers were later included in the design … seems a bit of a luxury really, considering that the pilot was never going to come back complaining of a sore bottom.
- Its fuselage was of circular cross section, this being easy to make, strong and bomb-like.
- The cockpit cover wasn't hinged, it was simply screwed on from

Nakajima Ki-115.

the outside as it would never have to open.

- It was designed to take an enormous variety of engines, so it could use up any spares that happened to be knocking around, although in practice only one type of engine was used.

- It was built from 'non-strategic' materials, meaning mainly wood, sealing wax, old beer bottles and string.

- The Imperial Japanese Navy gave it the rather poetic name of 'Wisteria Blossom'. Maybe this was a comfort to the pilot on his last mission.

- After initial testing, the plane was fitted with two rockets for extra speed, presumably to ensure the pilot met his maker before he had time to change his mind.

YOKOSUKA MXY7 OHKA

CHERRY BLOSSOM SOUNDS MUCH NICER THAN FLYING COFFIN

It is interesting that both the Germans and the Japanese held their highly trained pilots in such huge esteem that they decided the best way to use them towards the end of the war was to strap them to flying bombs and invite them to steer themselves towards almost certain oblivion. There were, however, two important differences in their approach.

The Germans did provide the pilots with at least a nominal chance of survival. On the Fieseler Fl 103R-IV Reichenberg, for example, the cockpit roof was removable (in theory at least, provided the pilot remembered to take along a socket set, a crowbar, a hammer and a set of chisels) and the pilots were given parachutes. The Japanese, by contrast, dispensed with such frippery. On the Ohka the cockpit roof was bolted down from the outside. But by way of compensation they did name their flying coffin Ohka, which means 'cherry blossom' and sounds much nicer than Reichenberg. This must have been such a great comfort for the victim, sorry pilot, in those final few seconds. The Allies apparently gave the Ohka the nickname 'Baka', meaning 'idiot' in Japanese.

There was one other serious drawback to the whole concept, however. The Ohka had a pathetic range of just 36km, which meant it had to be carried to within range of its target by a large bomber. The bomber of choice was none other than the Mitsubishi G4M Betty, itself featured earlier as the flying petrol bomb. So many of the poor Ohka pilots were not blown to pieces in the final attack but were fried alive when their parent G4M blew up above them. Fried alive or blown to pieces … difficult choice that.

Crew	1
Length	6.06m (19ft 11in)
Wingspan	5.12m (16ft 10in)
Height	1.16m (3ft 10in)
Wing area	6.0m²
Weight empty	440kg (968lb)
Gross weight	2,140kg (4,708lb)
Engines	3 x Type 4 Mark 1 Model 20 rocket motors
Cruising speed	it didn't cruise
Max speed	1,040kph (650mph) in a dive
Range	36km
Endurance	4.4 minutes
Armament	1,200kg Ammonal warhead

Yokosuka MXY7
Ohka.

TUPOLEV TU-144

CONCORDSKI ... HOW TO GET JUST ABOUT EVERYTHING WRONG

The Tu-144 was Russia's answer to Concorde. The slight problem is that the Russians clearly didn't understand the question. Although in flight it looked remarkably similar to Concorde, and quite elegant, there were so many odd features about this aircraft that it warrants inclusion in this book as 'strange'. In summary:

- Whereas Concorde made use of the superb Olympus turbojet, the Russians didn't have a turbojet powerful enough to push the Tu-144 through the sound barrier. So instead they used enormous turbofans. Slight problem: turbofans cannot take in air at supersonic speed, so the designers had to design baffles and things to actually slow the air down before it entered the engines. This was disastrous for fuel efficiency.
- Whereas Concorde only used afterburners for take-off and passing through the sound barrier, the Tu-144 only worked with afterburners on all the time because of the turbofans, disastrous for economy. It also made the aircraft so noisy it could almost be heard in neighbouring continents, and virtually no foreign airport would accept it.
- One Tu-144 crashed at the Paris Air Show in 1973, and another crashed whilst being delivered in 1978. After the second crash the passenger services ceased after just fifty-five scheduled flights.
- The cooling system for the outer skin of the aircraft, essential for supersonic flight, was so noisy that even passengers sitting next to each other could only converse by shouting. Two seats away and the only way to communicate was by written notes. The noise at the rear was so bad these seats were never used at all.
- What must be unique in aviation history is the limited use of the plane triggered by the fear of killing too many passengers! Such was the level of fear at top government levels that it was only ever used on one route. And fearful of crashes they also limited it to just one flight

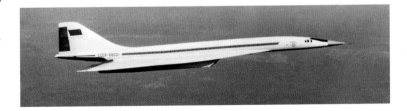

Tupolev Tu-144. (Wikimedia Commons courtesy of RIA Novosti)

Crew	3
Victim capacity	140 but in practice limited to 70
Length	65.5m (214ft 11in)
Wingspan	28.8m (94ft 6in)
Height	12.5m (41ft 0in)
Weight empty	99,200kg (218,240lb)
Weight loaded	125,000kg (275,000lb)
Engines	4 x Kuznetsov NK-144 turbofan
Power	200kN (44,962lbf) each
Max speed	2,120kph
Ceiling	20,000m

per week, the minimum to allow them to claim a 'regular' service. Passenger numbers were also limited to a maximum of seventy, half the capacity of 140, as they were afraid of losing too many people in one go in the event of a crash. However, it must have been Politburo logic that killing 140 would be so infinitely worse than killing a mere seventy.

- On one notable flight on 25 January 1978, on a plane unfortunately carrying many foreign journalists, twenty-two of the twenty-four critical on-board systems failed before take-off, but to avoid embarrassment the flight continued. Warning lights came on signalling failure of all the landing gear, triggering an ear-splitting warning siren immediately after take-off, which couldn't be turned off, so the crew had to stuff a pillow into the siren. In the end the plane landed safely, but apparently the premier Brezhnev had been constantly updated throughout the flight about the developing situation.

- The loss of two planes during a career that only included fifty-five scheduled flights must be a record, albeit a very sad one.

- The safety issue with the Tu-114 became so severe that, after it had experienced 226 technical failures in just 180 hours' flying, the chief designer, Alexei Tupolev, and two USSR aviation vice-ministers had to inspect each aircraft before every flight to make sure it was safe to fly that day (which, of course, it never really was).

- Oh, and finally, the interior. I've been on board a Tu-144, the one on display at Sinsheim Museum in Germany. The interior trim takes some believing. It makes a typical early 1950s British sitting room look positively cutting-edge chic!

- For totally deaf, antisocial, danger-loving retro-freaks, the Tu-144 was perfect-ski!

It may be a little unfair to say the Starfighter was perfectly designed to kill its pilots. But, designed or not, it made a damned good job of doing so. The German Air Force lost a staggering 30 per cent of their Starfighters through accidents. In Canada it was even worse, with 50 per cent being lost.

However, to be fair, it wasn't just the aircraft's fault. Well, having said that, it largely was. The aircraft had such tiny wings that a high airspeed had to be maintained at all times, otherwise the F-104 would adopt all the finer flying characteristics of a rubbish skip. A by-product of this high-speed requirement was a tendency, with the slightest movement of the joystick, to flip up and stall. All this wasn't helped by the unreliability of the new General Electric J79 engine,

Crew	1
Length	16.66m (54ft 7in)
Wingspan	6.36m (20ft 10in)
Height	4.09m (13ft 5in)
Weight empty	6,350kg (13,970lb)
Weight loaded	9,365kg (20,603lb)
Engine	1 x General Electric J79-GE-11A
Thrust	48kN (10,000lbf) dry
	69kN (15,600lbf) with afterburner
Max speed	2,137kph (Mach 2.01)
Range	2,623km
Ceiling	15,000m
Number built	2,575

Lockheed F-104
Starfighter.

which had a nasty habit of suddenly depriving the pilot of his essential high speed to remain airborne.

Oh, and we must not forget one other unique feature of the F-104. The ejector seat projected the pilot downwards not upwards, which was not exactly a comforting thought for the pilot when he remembered most engine failures occurred at low altitudes.

Add to all these woes:

- Variable thrust nozzles that had a mind of their own.

- Afterburner blow out on take-off.
- Non-ignition of the afterburners at the critical moment of take-off.
- Severe nose wheel shimmy on landing, which could result in the plane flipping onto its back.
- Flaps that sometimes worked in the wrong direction.
- High incidence of fatigue failure in the wings due to the very high loading because of their tiny size.

And then give the planes to Luftwaffe pilots who had not flown since the war apart from a brief refresher course, and the outcome might have been predictable.

In spite of all its troubles, when it managed to remain airborne, the F-104 was able to distinguish itself. It was the first aircraft ever to hold speed and altitude records at the same time. On 16 May 1958 it achieved a record 1,404.19mph, having earlier on 7 May achieved an altitude record of 91,243ft. Its record descents are less well documented or celebrated, however.

FOCKE-ACHGELIS FA 330

GIVES A WHOLE NEW MEANING TO THE TERM 'SITTING DUCK' ... OR SHOULD IT BE FLYING DUCK?

The Focke-Achgelis Fa 330 was not in fact a powered aircraft but what is called a 'rotary wing kite', in effect an autogyro without a motor. They were towed behind German U-boats at altitude to spot enemy vessels from a distance.

Now it is not difficult to see a slight flaw in the whole concept. Submarines are 'stealth' vessels, which spend a lot of time hidden under the water, and when on the surface

FA 330 Autogyro.

Crew	1
Length	4.42m (14ft 6in)
Rotor diameter	7.32m (24ft 0in)
Weight empty	68kg (150lb)
Engine	None
Power	0kW (0hp)
Max speed	40kph (25mph)
Min speed	27kph (17mph)
Range	infinite
Endurance	limitless
Ceiling	150m (500ft)

offer a low discreet profile so they are not easily seen. The downside is that their crew cannot see very far either. However, short of hoisting a flag saying 'Here we are, come and get us!', discharging colourful fireworks and playing 'Deutschland, Deutschland uber alles' through vast loudspeakers on the deck, it would be hard to think of a better way to be spotted out on the open seas than dragging a rotary wing kite at the end of a 150m (500ft) cable.

At an altitude of 150m the sitting duck – sorry, observer – could see for around 46km (25 miles). The downside was that he could also be seen by Allied shipping at 46km.

I don't know how easy the Germans found it to get volunteers to sit strapped in a seat 500ft above a moving U-boat. Maybe none of the 'observers' survived to enlighten us. At least nine Fa 330s survive today in museums.

DIVINE INTERVENTION OR MAGIC MUSHROOMS?

Looking at some of the amazingly original and way-out aircraft that have made it from the drawing board to the airfield, it is hard not to come to the conclusion that either divine intervention has taken place, or that in the offices of some aircraft manufacturers the designers are no strangers to 'magic mushrooms' with an unprecedented potency. Maybe God works part-time in some design offices, or perhaps certain substances are injected into the air conditioning in order to promote communal creativity. Whatever, some of the aircraft featured in this section were certainly the products of designers who had either an unprecedented level of creativity or who simply had one wheel short of a full undercarriage.

UTIAS ORNITHOPTER NO. 1

MAYBE BEST TO LEAVE WING FLAPPING TO BIRDS

An 'ornithopter' is an aircraft that tries to imitate the flight of a bird by having flapping wings, rather than using simple fixed aerofoils. That this was a stupid concept from the start should have been highlighted by the fact that Leonardo da Vinci had proposed it 500 years ago. Leonardo may have been a reasonable painter, but he was an awful engineer. All his 'inventions' to do with aviation were total crap. For example his design for a 'helicopter' firstly would never have worked, and if it had worked would only ever have gone vertically up and down … not very useful in practice. In any case the Chinese had a children's toy that actually worked as a simple helicopter 2,000 years earlier.

But this heritage has not put people off the idea of imitating birds. It is tempting to say that those pursuing this dubious goal must be a little bird-brained.

Having said all that, the UTIAS Ornithopter No. 1 actually did fly. Well, when I say 'fly', on 8 July 2006 it rose a few inches into the air for fourteen seconds travelling around 300m. However, whether the flight was the result of the flapping wings or more the result of strapping an auxiliary jet engine to the craft is somewhat debatable. I suspect a dead pigeon might fly a few hundred metres if you tied a jet engine to its backside, without one single wing flap. It is likely that the wing flapping on the Ornithopter actually hindered rather than helped the thing to take off.

UTIAS Ornithopter.

Crew	1 (preferably an ornithologist not too keen on travel)
Length	7.47m (24ft 6in)
Wingspan	12.56m (41ft 2in)
Gross weight	322kg (708lb)
Engine	1 x Konig SC-430
Power	18kW (24hp)
Cruising speed	82kph
Ceiling	15cm
Range	300m

AEROVIRONMENT HELIOS

IT WILL FLY FOREVER ... BUT BEST TO GET HOME BEFORE IT GOES DARK

AeroVironment Inc. is a high-tech company based in Monrovia and Simi Valley in California, specialising in energy systems, electric vehicles and unmanned aerial vehicles. The company is probably best known for its human-powered Gossamer Condor, the first successful human-powered aircraft, and for the Gossamer Albatross, the craft which in 1979 flew 37km across the English Channel. The company went on to build the Gossamer Penguin, a solar-powered variant of the Albatross. All great stuff.

Then one day, after I presume a 'special' lunch, the design team came up with the idea of the Helios, shown on the right in the photograph. It seemed logical that day that the Helios should have fourteen propellers and five fuselages, and that with a wingspan of 247ft it should be around twenty times wider than it is long. It must be the floppiest aircraft ever to fly. It is certainly not the fastest, with a top speed of around 25mph. The whole upper surface of the enormous wing is covered with photocells.

Having said all that, the solar-cell- and fuel-cell-powered craft has set a world altitude record for propeller-driven flight at 29,524m. It was intended as the prototype of a sort of 'atmospheric satellite', which could fly almost indefinitely powered by the sun although a small technical detail called 'night time' posed a few problems. An on-board battery did allow around two to four hours flight in darkness, but probably wise to head home before sunset. Later developments have focused on the use of liquid hydrogen fuel cells rather than solar cells.

AeroVironment Helios.

LOCKHEED MARTIN P-791

A CROSS BETWEEN AN AIRCRAFT, AN AIRSHIP AND A SOAP DISPENSER

I suspect that the designer of the P-791 arrived at work as normal one miserable Monday morning and started preliminary designs for a normal aircraft – you know the sort of thing: two wings, a tail, a couple of engines and some space in between for passengers or freight. Clearly the miserable weather got to him, and at lunchtime he decided to cheer himself up with a 'mushroom' omelette.

Returning somewhat revived to the drawing board, he'd forgotten whether he was meant to be designing an aircraft, a whoopee cushion, or a soap dispenser for use in a shower ... hence the four large suction pads. As the afternoon wore on the effects of the mushrooms started wearing off, and the idea started to look a little less clever.

In order to save his job, the outlandish design became an aerostatic/ aerodynamic hybrid airship, a technical description he knew his boss wouldn't understand, and the four suction pads became mini hovercraft to ensure a smooth landing. Evidently his job also had a smooth landing, and the concept was taken up quite seriously by the company. The future of the magic omelettes is less clear.

Its first flight was on 31 January 2006 at the company's flight-test facility at the Palmdale Air Force Base. As a hybrid vehicle, part of the weight is carried by the three gas-filled compartments, and part by the normal aerodynamic lift. Originally it was intended for military use, but the contract was lost to competitor Northrop and the fancy soap dispenser is now being developed for civilian use, as a cargo aircraft with a capacity of around 20 tonnes.

Technical details are difficult to obtain ... well, impossible, actually.

Lockheed Martin P-791.

47

FLETTNER PLANE 921-V

WHY BOTHER WITH WINGS WHEN A COUPLE OF ROTATING OIL DRUMS WILL DO?

The Flettner Plane 921-V must be a strong candidate for the strangest aircraft of all time. It had no wings at all. Instead it uses a pair of what were called Flettner Rotors. Working according to what is known as the Magnus Effect, these rotating drums generate an aerodynamic lift when moved through the air. In fact the principle is very much like that used on the bouncing bomb designed by Barnes Wallace.

Anton Flettner first used the principle on the boat shown in the first photograph. This boat was actually quite successful in some ways, and completed trouble-free journeys across the North Sea in 1925, and later in 1926 across the Atlantic. The slight drawback was that the large engines spinning the 15m-tall drums would have worked infinitely more efficiently driving simple propeller screws.

Anyway, possibly after an extended liquid lunch, Flettner decided that if it worked at sea it would also work in the air. And so the wingless Flettner Plane 921-V came into being.

It wasn't a complete failure, as it did fly … once. One potentially serious drawback of the Flettner idea is that the cylinders provide lift only when they are rotating quickly and moving forwards through the air. This means the engine must power both the drums and a propeller. Should the engine stop, and the drums cease rotating, they then provide about as much lift as a wheelbarrow. Even a helicopter will glide after a fashion when the engine stops, as the rotor continues turning and providing some lift, as with an autogyro. When Flettners drums stop rotating they become … well, just drums.

Flettner ship.

Flettner Rotor Aircraft.

CENTRAL HYDROFOIL DESIGN BUREAU'S KORABL MAKET
BETTER KNOWN AS THE CASPIAN SEA MONSTER

The Caspian Sea Monster, as it became known in the West, is definitely one of my personal favourite strange 'aircraft'. I put aircraft in inverted commas for a good reason. In many ways it was neither a plane nor a boat. It seems not even the Russians could decide. It was documented as a marine vessel, when it was 'launched' a bottle of champagne was broken against its fuselage, it displayed the Soviet Navy flag and was assigned to the Soviet Navy. Yet it was piloted by air force pilots, and certainly flew through the air, albeit at an altitude of between 4 and 14m. It bore the mark 'KM', which actually meant Korabl Maket, or 'prototype ship' in Russian. But in the West KM quickly became 'Kaspian Monster', and the name stuck.

Designed in 1964–65, the Caspian Sea Monster first came to the West's attention when spy planes spotted a truly massive 'thing' flying over the Caspian Sea. What the 'thing' was wasn't understood for some time, but its scale was clear. With a length of 92m, and a maximum take-off weight of an incredible 544 tonnes, it was by far the largest aircraft in the world until the Antonov An-225. Curiously, however, the spy plane cameras could not detect any altitude at all for the Monster. It seemed to be travelling at great speed at zero height. Either the instruments were faulty, or it was indeed a true monster!

Technically it was a ground-effect aircraft, which means it flew so low that the downdraft from the wings pushed against the water, much like a hovercraft, giving much greater lift than the simple aerofoil effect. In the technical language

Korabl Maket or Caspian Sea Monster.

of the aeronautical engineer, this means it could lift shit loads of stuff, efficiently, at great speed.

KM testing started in 1966 on the Caspian Sea near Kaspiysk, Dagestan. The very first flight was performed by Vladimir Loginov and Rostislav Alexeyev, the designer. This was very unusual as most Soviet aircraft designers never piloted their own designs; looking at some aircraft like the Tu-144 it's easy to understand why! All test flights were conducted under the patronage of the Ministry of Shipbuilding Industry.

The Monster was tested on the Caspian Sea for fifteen years, up until 1980. Then in 1980 a pilot error caused the plane to crash, fortunately with no human casualties. However, the Monster was too heavy to retrieve from its watery grave, which is such a great shame. Although the Monster itself no longer survives, smaller ground effect aircraft of similar design can still be seen in Russia.

Of course, the Americans never want to be outdone by the Russians, and in 2002 they revealed a concept for a 1,500-tonne capacity ground-effect aircraft, with a length of 122m and a wingspan of 152m. The so-called Boeing Pelican would have dwarfed the Caspian Sea Monster. However, it remained only a concept, and nothing further has been seen or heard of the Pelican since. Maybe it's flown the nest.

Crew	Not known
Length	92m (301ft 10in)
Wingspan	37.6m (123ft 4in)
Height	21.8m (71ft 6in)
Weight empty	240,000kg (528,000lb)
Weight loaded	544,000kg (1,196,800lb)
Engines	10 x Dobrynin VD-7 turbojets
Thrust	127.53kN (28,670lbf) each
Cruising speed	430kph
Max speed	500kph
Range	1,500km
Altitude	4–14m
Max sea state	1.2m

CONVAIR NC-131H TIFS

NOW THAT REALLY IS A FLIGHT SIMULATOR!

A quick look at the photograph might suggest the Convair NC-131H TIFS is taking off with another aircraft in the background. But no, that is one aircraft. It does, however, require some explanation.

Flight simulators are specially designed earth-bound environments where trainee pilots can safely kill themselves without the inconvenience of blood, guts, wreckage and million-pound lawsuits.

However, after reinforcing their creative juices with some highly classified substance, the designers at Convair decided earth-bound simulators were simply too whimpish for training 'real' pilots. Surely much better to strap the simulator onto the front of a real aeroplane and show the trainees what real fright is like. By the way, the TIFS in the name stands for Total In-Fright, sorry In-*Flight*, Simulator. I do wonder whether they actually told the trainee pilots their 'simulator' was strapped to the front of a real plane, or whether they were ushered in the dark into the cockpit and only realised they were really in the air when the 'projected' landscape started to look just a tad too realistic.

The Convair 131 itself was about as mundane a 1950s aircraft as you could get, until the simulator was attached to the front.

Crew	4 (plus 1 terrified trainee)
Length	24.1m + simulator (79ft 0in +)
Wingspan	32.1m (105ft 4in)
Height	8.59m (28ft 2in)
Weight empty	13,294kg (29,247lb)
Weight loaded	21,363kg (46,999lb)
Engines	2 x Pratt & Whitney 18-cyl 'Double Wasp'
Power	1,865kW (2,500hp) each
Cruising speed	409kph
Max speed	472kph
Range	725km
Altitude	7,470m

Convair NC-131H Total In Flight Simulator.

AMES DRYDEN AD1 OBLIQUE WING

KEEP AERONAUTICAL ENGINEERS AWAY FROM THE 'CERTAIN SUBSTANCES'

Sometimes we'll see a plane and just wonder what the designer must have been 'on' when he or she designed it. Such is the case with the Ames Dryden AD1 Oblique Wing.

We're familiar with helicopters, with rotating wings, and swing-wing planes where both wings hinge backwards for fast flight. But the AD1 is fundamentally different. The wings can rotate up to 60°, but in 'opposite' directions because it's in one piece.

My first thought was that the designer built this craft in a building where the door was narrower than the wingspan, so in order to get it outside he had to turn the wing. By then the glue had set, so he ended up with this strange object. My second thought was that the designer was simply on the funny mushrooms again, and to him the wing looked perfectly normal.

I'm not an aeronautical engineer, but my simple understanding of physics would suggest to me that when the wing is rotated there will be a turning moment either forcing a nose dive, or a steep climb and a potential stall. If the idea had caught on, and we had large passenger aircraft like this, I can imagine the passengers being just a tad scared when they looked out of one side and saw a wing, then looked out of the other side and saw ... well, nothing!

Ames Dryden AD1 Oblique Wing.

Crew	1
Length	11.83m (38ft 9in)
Wingspan	9.85m (unswept) 4.93m (swept)
	32ft 4in (unswept) 16ft 2in (swept)
Height	2.06m (6ft 9in)
Weight empty	658kg (1,448lb)
Weight loaded	973kg (2,141lb)
Engines	2 x Microturbo TRS-18 turbojets
Power	0.98kN (220lbf) each
Fuel capacity	300 litres
Max speed	322kph
Ceiling	3,658m

FANWING

INSPIRED BY A COMBINE HARVESTER OR CYLINDER MOWER?

Fanwing is an ingenious flying concept conceived by Patrick Peebles, an American citizen based in the UK. Instead of a conventional wing, it uses a partially enclosed horizontal fan to create both lift and forward thrust. The fan extends the entire width of the 'wing', offers very short take-offs and landings, and is very quiet and efficient. To date the technology has been proven with a flying scale model, backed by a UK government SMART Award, and the concept is being developed further with help from an EU-funded research programme.

By Patrick Peebles' own admission it does bear more than a slight resemblance to a combine harvester, or a cylinder mower, but is faster than both and can achieve a somewhat greater altitude. Maybe very high-speed grass cutting or harvesting very tall crops could provide a lucrative sideline for the business. It could also sound the death knell for the slow, old-fashioned Flymo.

The company is now working on a manned version of Fanwing, and ultimately they envisage a cargo-carrying version, as shown in the artist's impression in the second

Fanwing. (Photos copyright FanWing Ltd; Projected images by Adrian Mann, copyright FanWing Ltd)

53

Fanwing. (Photos copyright FanWing Ltd; Projected images by Adrian Mann, copyright FanWing Ltd)

photograph. This would be capable of carrying a full-sized container, and could operate from extremely short runways, possibly as short as three times the aircraft's own length, ideal for operation in remote or under-developed parts of the world.

Fanwing has been described as 'One of the few truly new aircraft since the Wright Brothers' by the *New York Times*. That cannot be disputed. In addition to cargo carrying, it has potential for fire-fighting, crop dusting, short-haul passenger services, military applications, and search and rescue. A strange aircraft yes, but in the best possible way!

Fanwing Inspiration.

EDGLEY OPTICA

WHAT WAS THE DESIGNER 'ON' WHEN HE DESIGNED THE 'BUG EYE'?

Looking at the Optica, which seems to have been inspired by a cross between a goldfish bowl, a dragonfly and an outsize toilet roll. It is certainly different, to put it mildly. It has been nicknamed the 'bug eye' for obvious reasons.

The Optica started life in 1974 when John Edgley founded Edgley Aircraft Limited. The Optica was unusual in having a fully glazed forward cabin, offering 270° panoramic vision and almost vertical downward vision for both the pilot and the passengers; not something for those scared of heights. The aircraft has twin booms with twin rudders mounted in an outside tailplane, and the flat-6 Lycoming engine is mounted inside the toilet roll, sorry duct, driving a large fan. The large ducted fan makes it a very quiet aircraft, and also helps it fly at very low speeds when needed, as slow as 67mph before the risk of a stall.

Although twenty production Opticas have been made, ten were destroyed in an arson attack on the factory, and three have been written off in accidents, giving a rather low survival rate of 35 per cent.

Crew	1
Passengers	2
Length	8.15m (26ft 9in)
Wingspan	12.0m (39ft 4in)
Weight empty	948kg (2,090lb)
Weight loaded	1,315kg (2,900lb)
Engine	1 x Textron Lycoming IO-540-V4A5S flat-6
Power	194kW (200hp)
Cruising speed	130kph (81mph)
Max speed	213kph (132mph)
Stall speed	108kph (67mph)
Range	1,056km (656 miles)
Ceiling	4,275m (14,000ft)
Number built	20 + 1 prototype

Edgley Optica.

LLOYD LUFTKREUZER

IT SHOULD PERHAPS HAVE BEEN CALLED LLOYD DAFTKREUZER

Few aircraft look as though the designers got nearly everything wrong, but in the case of the Lloyd Daftkreuzer, sorry Luftkreuzer, they came very close.

The Luftkreuzer was the product of the Hungarian Lloyd Aircraft and Motor Works Inc., a name which looks much more impressive written in Hungarian. After producing a number of fairly normal-looking aircraft, they produced the Lloyd FJ 40.05, which solved the problem of firing a gun forwards on a single propeller aircraft by locating the gunner high up in a turret so he could fire over the top of the prop. The designers at Lloyd obviously liked this idea, because when they came to build the triple-engined Luftkreuzer in 1916 they retained the tall turret, even though there was no central propeller to shoot over. Indeed they must have liked the concept so much that they also added a gondola below the aircraft for the bomb aimer. And just to make the whole design bonkers they added a third wing below that.

The Luftkreuzer, or Air Cruiser, had three engines. The main engine was a Daimler 300hp 12-cylinder driving a central pusher propeller, and the other two, mounted either side of the fuselage, were Daimler 160hp 6-cylinder units. The Luftkreuzer had a few small technical faults:

- Because of the gunner's turret the pilot couldn't see forwards at all.
- In order to accommodate the bomb aimer's gondola the whole contraption was raised to such a height it was completely unstable.
- The turret and gondola made the aircraft impossibly nose heavy.
- The two forward-facing propellers rotated in the same direction, thereby doubling the gyroscopic effect that normally is cancelled out on twin-engined aircraft.
- On the ground the tail of the aircraft had to be propped up on a trestle, which posed just a few technical problems concerning take-off.
- In fact there is no evidence that the Air Cruiser ever took to the air. All surviving photographs show it on the ground propped up on its trestle. Perhaps they should have added wheels to the trestle to allow it to taxi for take-off.

Apart from these quite trivial issues, and the fact that it couldn't actually fly, the Luftkreuzer represented a monumental leap forward for the Austro-Hungarian Empire's aeronautical industry.

Lloyd Luftkreuzer.

DON'T LET THE AIRCRAFT DESIGNERS GO FOR A PUB LUNCH

We've all been there. It's a hot summer's day and we've been slaving away since 8.30. Now it's 12.30 and time to think about some lunch. The choice is either the canteen or a sandwich at the desk. But no, there is an alternative … the pub. Of course this is frowned upon by 'management', but it is a special occasion. OK, well it's not really a special occasion, but we can invent one … it's someone's birthday, the dog has had puppies, the cat hasn't been run over by an ice-cream van, you've won the lottery, the world didn't end at 9.37 last Monday as predicted by the mystic looking Indian guy in the corner shop … so a trip to the pub is suddenly legit. But as we know the 'just one drink as I'm designing the next generation of super-mega-euro-fighter' soon becomes 'OK, just one more, it's only a ******* plane after all.' And the result is inevitable.

GYROFLUG SPEED CANARD

THE 1943 CURTISS ASCENDER REINCARNATED

Back in the mid 1940s a curious aircraft took to the sky called the Curtis XP55 Ascender. It was nicknamed the 'Arse-ender' because of its pusher design. I suspect it owes part of its strange design to a 'liquid lunch'. In the morning the designer had outlined a highly conventional fuselage, and after his pre-prandial exertion felt the need for a four-pint lunch, washed down by the odd rye whisky or eight.

On returning to the drawing board in the afternoon, the designer was in a jolly, rather flippant mood and decided to:

- Put the engine at the back for a bit of a lark.
- Give it two tails, one pointing up and one pointing down.
- Give it swept wings to make it look a little racy, although with a top speed of just 390mph it scarcely needed them.
- Put the tailplane at the front for a laugh.
- Give the pilot a good view by modelling the cockpit on a small greenhouse.

Crew	1
Passengers	1
Length	4.7m (15ft 5in)
Wingspan	7.77m (25ft 6in)
Height	1.81m (5ft 11in)
Weight empty	440kg (968lb)
Weight loaded	815kg (1,793lb)
Engine	1 x Avco Lycoming O-320-D1A
Power	120kW (161hp)
Max speed	295kph
Range	1,325km
Altitude	5,640m
Number built	62 (by 1995)

So overall it looked like it had been built backwards. The Ascender didn't have a particularly good life. In November 1943 the first XP55 was being tested at high altitude for stall characteristics when … well, it stalled, suddenly flipped over and plummeted towards the ground. The pilot was able to bale out before the plane crashed and was destroyed. The third of the three XP55s crashed at an air display in Ohio, killing the pilot. The second of the prototypes survives and is on display at Air Zoo in Michigan. Unfortunately no good-quality photographs of it survive.

But scroll forward forty years, cross over the Atlantic, and we find the spirit of the Curtis XP55 reborn in Germany in the shape of the Gyroflug Speed Canard. The layout is very similar, with swept-back wings, small canard winglets on the nose, no proper tail, and an engine mounted at the back with a pusher propeller.

Gyroflug Speed Canard.

The main difference is that the Gyroflug is a two-seater, the plane having room for a brave passenger behind the pilot. As a result the fuselage looks to be all cockpit. In fact this long cockpit is basically taken from the Grob Twin Astir sailplane, where it looks more at home with a proper fuselage behind.

The Speed Canard has one claim to fame. Constructed throughout of composite materials, it is the first composite canard design to achieve airworthiness certification anywhere in the world. It has also been fairly successful commercially, with sixty-two built.

ROCKWELL XFV-12

A PLANE DEFEATED BY THE LAWS OF GRAVITY

The XFV-12 was a brave attempt to incorporate the Mach 2 speed and missile capability of the McDonnell Douglas F-4 Phantom into a vertical take-off aircraft. On paper the specification looked superior to that of the Hawker Siddeley Harrier, but there was one rather serious snag: it was actually unable to take off vertically, in spite of the engine generating more thrust than the plane weighed. So, basically, it was Gravity 1: Rockwell 0.

The plane's rather strange design may not have helped. I can only presume the designer had completed the wings before going to the pub for lunch, and on his return he forgot he'd already done the wings and so did them a second time. Hence the aircraft ended up with two sets of wings. The inebriated designer then realised that, after building two sets of wings, there'd be no money left for the tail, so it didn't get one. Sobering up later he decided that maybe a pair of tiny tailplanes could be afforded but placed them on the end of the rear set of wings.

Problems arose immediately. The craft simply would not rise vertically, maybe just a marginally important feature of a vertical take-off aircraft. To solve this more nozzles were fitted in both sets of wings, but then the ducting became so long and complex that by the time the exhaust eventually managed to find an escape route from the aircraft it was so tired it was only capable of lifting 75 per cent of the aircraft's weight.

Just one prototype was completed. A second was never finished and the whole project was cancelled. So came to an end the NQVTOL (Not Quite Vertical Take Off & Landing) programme.

Crew	1
Length	13.4m (44ft 0in)
Wingspan	8.7m (28ft 7in)
Weight empty	6,259kg (13,770lb)
Weight loaded	8,850kg (19470lb)
Engine	1 x Pratt & Whitney F401 afterburning turbofan
Thrust	133kN (30,000lbf)
Max speed	Mach 2.2–2.4
Armament	1 x 20mm M61 Vulcan cannon
	2 x AIM-7 Sparrow missiles
	2 x AIM-9L Sidewinder missiles
Number built	2

Rockwell XFV-12.

RUTAN VARIEZE

A DIY AIRCRAFT WITH ONE UNIQUE FEATURE

Burt Rutan was a prolific designer of unusual aircraft, many designed for DIY enthusiasts to build for themselves. In that role it has certainly been a success, with over 800 having been built. However, home build is clearly not without its problems. Of the 800 or so believed to have been built, 130 have crashed, forty-six with fatal results. Maybe building aircraft is a little more complex than putting up pictures or repairing a dripping tap.

It is also evident that there must be hundreds of suburban garages with part-built Variezes inside. It is believed around 2,000 were under construction by 1980, but well under half have ever seen the light of day. Given the high accident rate that may be no bad thing.

The Varieze, first flown in 1975, was unconventional with its canard wings and pusher propeller, and its mouldless composite construction was ideal for home assembly. But what really made it unusual was the nose wheel. In the photograph it appears to have no nose wheel at all. In fact this is not the case. It does have an extendable nose wheel for take-off and landing, but this has to be retracted on the ground before the pilot gets out. If not the plane apparently tips over backward – not too good for the rear propeller. The plane in the photograph is in what is known as the 'parking position'.

The sale of plans for the Varieze ceased in 1985, but at the time it was, at least in numbers sold if not safety, by far the most successful home-build aircraft in the world.

Crew	1
Length	4.32m (14ft 2in)
Wingspan	6.77m (22ft 3in)
Weight empty	263kg (579lb)
Weight loaded	476kg (1,047lb)
Engine	1 x Continental O-200-B air-cooled flat four
Power	75kW (100hp)
Cruising speed	266kph
Max speed	314kph
Stall speed	89kph
Range	1,368km
Number built	around 800

Rutan Varieze.

The Model 202 Boomerang was another highly original design from Burt Rutan. Although from the photograph it looks like a plane designed by two people who never met, one working from the left wing tip and the other from the right, there was apparently a logic behind the highly asymmetrical appearance. And by the way, although the photo seems to have been cut off just below the port tailplane, that is what it actually looked like. It really was that asymmetrical.

The Boomerang was designed to be a multi-engine aircraft that would not become dangerous to fly in the event of the failure of one engine. It was designed around the Beechcraft Baron 58 specification, one of the most numerous and successful twin-engine civilian aircraft. Apparently, apart perhaps from scaring onlookers and dogs, the asymmetrical design allows the Boomerang to fly faster than the Baron but using the same engines, and carrying the same number of people.

The two engines on the Boomerang are identical, but the starboard engine

Crew	1
Passengers	4 (or 500kg cabin payload)
Length	9.36m (30ft 8in)
Wingspan	11.12m (36ft 6in)
Weight empty	1,070kg (2,354lb)
Weight loaded	1,900kg (4,180lb)
Engines	1 x Lycoming TIO-360-A1B 4-cylinder
	1 x Lycoming TIO-360-C1A6D 4-cylinder
Power	149kW and 157kW (200hp and 210hp)
Cruising speed	402kph
Max speed	530kph
Stall speed	130kph
Range	3,780km
Number built	1

is tuned to produce 8kW more than the port engine. In a symmetrical design this would result in the plane going round in circles, but on the Boomerang the power differential balances the design. Clever!

The only Boomerang built was fully restored in 2011 and flown in a display as a tribute to Rutan.

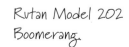

Rutan Model 202 Boomerang.

GRUMMAN X-29

A PLANE DESIGNED TO BE UNCONTROLLABLE

It must have been a very heavy lunch indeed for the designers working on the X-29, for they managed to design an aircraft that was impossible for the pilot to fly.

Whatever the designers washed their lunch down with had a strange effect on them. They decided it would be an absolutely corking idea to put the wings on back to front. Such wings apparently cause 'aerolastic divergent twisting', which sounds like something men might suffer from if their Lycra cycling shorts are too tight, and is probably even worse than it sounds. To counter this the wings were made of light composite material, which created a further problem. The centre of gravity was so far behind the aerodynamic centre that the whole aircraft was intrinsically unstable, and liable at any moment to flick its nose up and plummet to the ground. This necessitated a complex computer system to make around forty corrections per second to the flight controls. To make sure this was 'safe' six computers were assigned to the task, any one of which could do the whole process.

Through some logic so complex and secret nobody understood it, it was believed that the inherent instability of the design would result in extreme manoeuvrability. This myth was kept going for years, apparently, although there was no supporting evidence for it throughout all the test flights.

Only two were built, completing 242 test flights between 1984 and 1991.

Crew	1
Length	14.7m (48ft 3in)
Wingspan	8.29m (27ft 2in)
Weight empty	6,260kg (13,772lb)
Weight loaded	8,070kg (17,754lb)
Engine	1 x General Electric F404 Turbofan
Thrust	71kN (16,000lbf)
Max speed	Mach 1.8
Range	560km
Ceiling	16,800m
Number built	2

MARTIN XB-51

IS THIS THE UGLIEST BOMBER OF ALL TIME?

The Martin XB-51 is strange mainly because it looks as though it was cobbled together in a rush one afternoon after the designers had returned very late from the pub. It is clear, for example, that earlier in the day they had forgotten the tiny detail of engines, and so hastily stuck them rather self-consciously on either side of the fuselage in a most unusual position. Then for luck they added a third engine under the tail, making it the only three-engine jet bomber of all time. With three engines and its high tail it has more in common with a Tristar or DC-10 than a normal bomber.

The designers also managed to come up with what must be the ugliest bomber ever designed, looking as though it was assembled from cardboard boxes and toilet roll tubes.

The XB-51 was first flown in 1949 and then was entered into a competition for a new night intruder/bomber, a need based on experience in the Korean War. Alongside the XB-51 in the contest were the Avro Canada CF-100 and the English Electric Canberra. In the end the Canberra won, maybe not least because, unlike the XB-51, it wasn't ugly enough to cause nightmares. However, Martin didn't lose out entirely, as they got the contract to build the Canberras for the US.

The XB-51 was also unusual in that it was developed to include Rocket-Assisted Take-Off (RATO), with four 954lbf-thrust rockets being deployed. The result was a rather impressive short take-off, as shown in the photograph. One advantage of this was that it removed the 'ugly duckling' more quickly from the gaze of unfortunate onlookers.

In the end only two were built, and both of these were lost in crashes.

Martin XB-51.

Crew	2
Length	25.9m (85ft 0in)
Wingspan	16.2m (53ft 2in)
Height	5.3m (17ft 5in)
Weight empty	13,419kg (29,522lb)
Weight loaded	25,366kg (55,805lb)
Engines	3 x General Electric J47-GE-13 turbojets (each 23kN (5,200lbf thrust)
	4x take-off rockets (each 4.24kN (954lbf thrust))
Max speed	1,040kph
Range	1,730km
Ceiling	12,300m
Armament	8 x 20mm cannon with 1,280 rounds
	8 x High Velocity Aerial Rockets (HVAR)
	2,000 bombs (10,400lb)
Number built	2

Martin XB-51
rocket-assisted
take-off.

65

DOUGLAS XB-42 MIXMASTER

A BOMBER THAT SOUNDS MORE LIKE A KITCHEN APPLIANCE

The XB-42 Mixmaster was 16.36m long. For the first 14 or so of these metres it looked like a normal plane. Then in the last 2m things went slightly crazy. It may be this rear part was the offspring of a post-prandial alcohol consumption episode.

Douglas XB-42 Mixmaster.

The Mixmaster was designed as a faster and cheaper replacement for the B-29 Superfortress. It was powered by two Allison V12 piston engines driving two enormous contra-rotating pusher propellers. This posed a problem. The propellers were so large there was a danger of them striking the runway during take-off. To prevent this a second, downward-pointing, tail fin was fitted. So whilst the propeller might remain safe, the extra tail could gouge a deep furrow in the tarmac if the angle at take-off was too steep.

The guns fired backwards from the trailing edges of the wings, because the designers believed the XB-42 would be so fast only a rear attack would be possible. It certainly was a fast plane, being capable of 488mph during testing. In December 1945 an XB-42 set a new transcontinental record, flying from Long Beach to Washington DC, 2,300miles, in five hours and seventeen minutes.

The XB-42 enjoyed very limited success. Only two were built, and they both suffered from instability, vibrations and poor engine cooling. The record-breaking plane was destroyed in a crash, whilst the surviving example was modified by having twin turbojets fitted in addition to the twin Allisons, making a very potent machine.

Final strange point … I can find no explanation for the name Mixmaster!

Crew	3
Length	16.36m (53ft 8in)
Wingspan	21.49m (70ft 6in)
Height	5.74m (18ft 10in)
Weight empty	9,475kg (20,845lb)
Weight loaded	16,194kg (35,627lb)
Engines	2 x Allison V-17 10-125 V12 piston engines
Power	988kW (1,325hp) each
Max speed	660kph
Range	2,895km
Ceiling	8,960m
Armament	6 x 12.7mm machine guns
	3,629kg of bombs
Number built	2

SUKHOI SU-47 BERKUT

WHAT ONE SHOT OF VODKA CAN DO

It is clear that the Soviets did not wish to remain behind in the 'strange aircraft war', so they also built aircraft partly back to front. The Sukhoi Su-47 Berkut is a good example. By the way, Berkut means golden eagle.

I assume the designers must have only indulged in one or two vodkas at lunchtime, because, wings apart, the Su-47 looks fairly normal. In addition to the main wings, it also

Sukhoi Su-47 Berkut.

Crew	1
Length	22.6m (74ft 2in)
Wingspan	15.16–16.70m (49ft 9in–54ft 1in)
Height	6.3m (20ft 8in)
Weight empty	16,375kg (36,025lb)
Weight loaded	25,000kg (55,000lb)
Engines	2 x Aviadvigatel D-30F6 afterburning turbofans
Thrust	83kN (18,700lbf) (142kN (32,000lbf) with afterburners) each
Max speed	Mach 1.65
Range	3,300km
Ceiling	18,000m
Armament	prototypes not armed
Number built	4

has canards upfront and tailplanes at the rear, so, in effect, three pairs of wings. It also worked very well, offering extremely high agility at subsonic speeds, whilst retaining manoeuvrability at supersonic speed.

Four prototypes were made.

BELL P-39 AIRACOBRA

THE PORSCHE 911 OF THE AIR?

Bell P-39 Airacobra.

The Bell P-39 Airacobra looks like a perfectly normal fighter plane. In most ways it was, and it was an extremely successful one, with 9,584 being built between 1941 and 1944. It was the principal fighter of the US Army Air Forces at the beginning of the Second World War, and during the war saw service with many other air forces, including the RAF and the Soviet Air Force.

Crew	1
Length	9.2m (30ft 2in)
Wingspan	10.4m (34ft 1in)
Height	3.8m (12ft 6in)
Weight empty	2,425kg (5,335lb)
Weight loaded	3,347kg (7,363lb)
Engine	1 x Allison V-17 10-85 V12 piston engine
Power	895kW (1,200hp)
Max speed	605kph
Range	840km
Ceiling	10,700m
Armament	1 x 37mm M4 cannon
	2 x 12.7mm Browning M2 machine guns
	4 x 7.6mm Browning M1919 machine guns
	up to 230kg bombs
Number built	9,584

So in what way was it strange? Well, just like a Porsche 911 the Airacobra was rear engined and powerful. The 1,200hp Allison V12 piston engine was located behind the cockpit, and drove the front propeller through a long and complicated set of shafts passing under the pilot's feet. It was also the first fighter to be fitted with a tricycle undercarriage.

The other unique feature of the Airacobra was that it was designed around the weaponry, not around the engine as most fighters were. The engine was moved to the back to make room for the massive 37mm Oldsmobile T9 cannon firing through the centre of the propeller hub. Although devastating when it worked, the T9 was prone to jamming and there was only room for a limited quantity of shells. The design also allowed the nose to be very streamlined.

In the early days the design caused the pilots a few concerns. The idea of the heavy engine just behind their heads, and the propshaft rotating at high speed just a short distance below their more sensitive areas, was a source of worry to some. But in operation neither of these proved to be a problem.

DORNIER DO 335
THE PUSH-ME/PULL-YOU FIGHTER

Dornier Do 335 A-6.

The Dornier Do 355 looks as though it was designed by an engineer who went to the pub at lunchtime, and then returned slightly worse for wear and designed a second nose complete with engine and propeller at the rear. As he sobered up later in the day he realised his mistake and made the rear 'nose' look a bit more like a tail by adding vestigial tail fins. Of course this was not actually true ... or was it?

In fact the design of the Do 335 did have certain advantages over more conventional twin-engined heavy fighters. The 'push-pull' configuration resulted in significantly less

Crew	1
Length	13.85m (45ft 5in)
Wingspan	13.8m (45ft 1in)
Weight empty	5,210kg (11,484lb)
Weight loaded	8,590kg (19,500lb)
Engines	2 x Daimler-Benz inverted V12
Power	1,287kW (1,726hp) each
Max speed	765kph (474 mph)
Range	1,160km (721 miles)
Ceiling	11,400m (37,400ft)
Armament	1 x 30mm MK103 cannon
	2 x 20mm MG151 synchronised cannon
Number built	around 13

drag than having the engines on the wings. In addition having an engine at both ends results in a better weight balance and improved handling. Claudius Dornier had used the tandem engine layout extensively in flying boats, including the gigantic Dornier X, which also features in this book.

There was, however, one small problem with the design. With one of the propellers mounted directly behind the cockpit, in the event of the pilot having to eject there was a serious risk of his being converted to mince meat. To get around this slight issue the aircraft was uniquely equipped with explosive bolts to blow the rear engine and propeller off before the pilot exited.

There was a two-seat trainer version, like the one shown in the photograph, which acquired the nickname Ameisenbar, meaning Anteater in German.

However, whilst the Luftwaffe was desperate to get its new heavy fighter into service, the development took so long that the war had ended before more than just a handful had been built.

KYUSHU J7W SHINDEN

DID THE DESIGNERS RUN OUT OF TIME?

The Kyushu J7W Shinden (Magnificent Lightning in Japanese) was a propeller-driven prototype fighter built to a canard design. The wings were attached to the tail section, and stabilisers were fitted on the nose to control flight.

In reality it looks as though the designer started at the front, designing a conventional fighter and got as far as the cockpit by lunchtime. However a longer than average lunch break meant he ran out of time when he returned to the drawing board and had to quickly finish off the rear. It looks as though it should have been twice as long.

The pusher propeller format was adopted because the Kyushu Aircraft Company had proposed a jet version once jet engines became more available. However, like the Dornier Do 335, the rear pusher propeller had one slight drawback: in the event of the pilot ejecting, the first thing he would encounter was the rapidly rotating blades. However, whilst Dornier took the precaution of designing an ejectable rear engine and propeller, Kyushu, following the philosophy of the Kamikazi, saw no need for such luxurious frippery.

The plan had been to build around 1,086 Shinden between April 1946 and March 1947. However, the end of the war in the Far East meant that only two prototypes were made.

Crew	1
Length	9.66m (31ft 8in)
Wingspan	11.11m (36ft 5in)
Weight empty	3,645kg (8,019lb)
Weight loaded	4,928kg (10,841lb)
Engine	1 x Mitsubishi Ha-43 18-cyl radial
Power	1,589kW (2,130hp)
Max speed	750kph (469mph)
Range	850km (531 miles)
Ceiling	12,000m (39,360ft)
Armament	4 x 30mm cannon
	4 x 30kg or 4 x 60kg bombs
Number built	2

PLANE BONKERS

Some aircraft are difficult to classify. Take the Avrocar for example. It resembles a car hubcap more than anything else. Alexander Lipisch's Aerodyne looks just like a dustbin, whilst the Blohm & Voss BV141 resembles a half-finished jigsaw of an aeroplane. It seemed logical to group these, and seven other daft designs, under a simple heading of 'plane bonkers'.

REPUBLIC XF-84H THUNDERSCREECH

THE NOISIEST AIRCRAFT EVER BUILT

The Republic XF-84H wasn't officially called the Thunderscreech. It gained this nickname, and others including Mighty Ear Banger, on account of its extraordinary noise. It is said that on take-off the aircraft could be heard up to 40km (25 miles) away.

The problems arose from the massive propeller. The 3.7m (12ft) prop turned at a constant speed, the thrust being adjusted by changing the pitch of the blades. However, even when idling, this meant that the tips of the blades were moving at Mach 1.18, generating a continuous sonic boom that radiated for hundreds of metres. The shock wave was powerful enough to knock a person over, and on one test run the sound from the Thunderscreech seriously incapacitated a pilot in a C-47 parked nearby. It was notorious for inducing severe nausea and headaches amongst ground crews, and at Edwards Air Force Base the pervasive noise and vibration seriously upset operations in the control tower, and posed a real risk to sensitive instrumentation.

The Thunderscreech was based on the F-84 turbojet fighter, with the jet being replaced by a 5,850hp (4,360kW) Allison XT40-A-1 turboprop unit. The engine was located behind the cockpit, and drove the prop through a long shaft. The aircraft was designed to address the need for a carrier-borne fighter that would not need catapult assistance.

The Thunderscreech was notable for its incredible acceleration and very high top speed. But it came with problems. The engine required thirty minutes to fully warm up, making it impractical as a front-line fighter, and it had serious stability issues. It had a reputation for 'snaking' in level flight at high speed, and there were persistent problems with vibration, engine failures, hydraulic failures and problems with the nose gear.

The Guinness Book of Records lists the Thunderscreech as the fastest propeller aircraft ever built, with a design speed of Mach 0.9 (1,080kph or 670mph). However, this speed is disputed and not supported

Crew	1
Length	15.67m (51ft 5in)
Wingspan	10.18m (33ft 5in)
Weight empty	8,132kg (17,892lb)
Weight loaded	12,293kg (27,046lb)
Engine	1 x Allison XT40-A-1 turboprop
Power	4,365kW (5,850hp)
Max speed	837kph (520mph)
Range	3,200km (2,000 miles)
Ceiling	14,600m (40,000ft)
Number built	2

by official records. The true top speed was probably around Mach 0.7 (840kph or 520mph), but this still makes it the fastest single-engined propeller aircraft of all time.

The ongoing problems resulted in the programme being cancelled in 1956. Only two were built, the second one making only four flights.

Republic XF-84H Thunderscreech.

AVRO CANADA AVROCAR

AN EXPENSIVE MILITARY FLYMO?

Crew	2
Diameter	5.5m (18ft 1in)
Wing area	254m²
Height	1.07m (3ft 6in)
Weight empty	1,361kg (2,994lb)
Weight loaded	2,522kg (5,548lb)
Engines	3 x Continental J69-T-9 turbojet
Power	2.9kN (652lbf) each
Max speed	(design) 483kph (actual) 56kph
Ceiling	(design) 3,048m (actual) 0.91m
Range	(design) 1,601km (actual) 127km

The first bizarre thing about the Avrocar is why it's called the Avrocar. It bears about as much resemblance to a car as I do to Brad Pitt; however, my wife informs me that in fact it does resemble a car rather more than I resemble Brad Pitt.

Let's face it, in reality this is about as close as it comes to being the flying saucer we all read about in comics when we were 14 years old. The concept was the idea of a designer called Jack Frost. (Yes, that really was his name … well, actually, it wasn't. His real name was John but everyone called him Jack.) He had wanted to improve on Frank Whittle's design of jet engine, and decided it would be better if the 'flame cans' were distributed radially around the outside of the centrifugal compressor. Slight problem: the thrust then emanates radially all round the engine, which is great for powering a Flymo lawn-mower but not quite so good for a military fighter plane. Being a stubborn man, Frost decided the logical thing to do was not to redesign his engine, but to radically change the whole concept of the aeroplane.

After a few design concepts, which looked more like car hubcaps than aircraft, he continued development work and eventually produced an Avrocar that could fly … I use that word 'fly' rather loosely, however.

Firstly there was the problem of the exhaust. The design had a slight weakness in that the exhaust was sucked back into the engine resulting in such high temperatures that the instruments in the cockpit started to melt with the heat. It can't have been too comfortable for the victim – sorry, pilot – either.

Secondly once the Avrocar rose above about 2ft off the ground a strange effect started. The air cushion that had built up when the craft first left the ground started leaking out in sort of enormous aerodynamic belches or farts causing the thing to bounce up and down on each of its undercarriage wheels in turn. This limited its maximum safe altitude to under 2ft. In tests it proved capable of crossing a ditch up to 6ft across and 18in deep, something that would hardly revolutionise field warfare. The project was dropped.

The Fact Box shows the rather embarrassing gap between the design performance and the actual performance. The verdict I suppose is simple: car hubcaps are not a good design cue for military aircraft, unless of course the grass on the battlefield needs a quick trim.

Avro Canada Avrocar.

ALEXANDER LIPPISCH AERODYNE

WAS ALEXANDER LIPPISCH ALLERGIC TO WINGS?

On the scale of strangeness, the Aerodyne sits somewhere near the very top. Most planes have two wings, and later we'll see that some had as many as 200 individual wings. The Aerodyne stands out because it has no wings at all.

The Aerodyne was powered by two co-axial shrouded propellers, the thrust from which could be deflected downwards by flaps for vertical take-off and landing. Control was by deflecting part of the airstream emerging from the end of the tail boom, and by flaps in the propeller slipstream.

Another slightly odd feature of the Aerodyne was that it had no cockpit at all. However, this was not a drawback as only unmanned flights were taken. The flight tests showed that the concept was quite workable. Indeed the Harrier jump jet incorporates some of Lippisch's ideas.

Alexander Lipisch Aerodyne.

BLOHM & VOSS BV 141

WERE THE DESIGNERS PLAYING A PRACTICAL JOKE ON THE LUFTWAFFE?

Looking at the Blohm & Voss BV 141, it's hard not to conclude that Herr Blohm and Herr Voss were having a good laugh at the expense of the Luftwaffe, who simply couldn't understand the joke.

The BV 141 is possibly the most asymmetrical plane ever built. Of course, rather than a joke, it could have been the result of some form of aeronautic dyslexia. Its single engine sat alongside the cockpit, which housed all the crew. Initially the tailplane was symmetrical, but they decided to scrap the tail wing on one side to give the rear-facing gunner a better view … and also, presumably, a lower risk of shooting off his own tail. Or maybe they'd decided that with twin tail wings the whole thing looked just a little too sensible. We'll never know.

Although the BV 141 is said to have performed 'well', this might have been a simple misunderstanding; when the test pilots were asked how the plane performed, maybe they started by saying 'Well …' followed by a long, pregnant pause whilst they tried to summon the words to describe how horrendously scary and awful the handling was, and explain the brown stains on their flying suit trousers.

Although twenty were made, it never entered full-scale production, for reasons which included the unavailability of the preferred engine, competition from the Focke-Wulf Fw 189, and the fact that most pilots didn't wish to appear as stupid prats in brown-stained trousers. Actually it might have been very effective against the Allied Spitfires and Hurricanes. It might have reduced the pilots to uncontrollable fits of laughter causing them to lose control.

Crew	3
Length	13.95m (45ft 9in)
Wingspan	17.45m (57ft 3in)
Height	3.6m (11ft 10in)
Weight empty	4,700kg (10,340lb)
Weight loaded	6,100kg (13,420lb)
Engine	1 x BMW 801A 14-cyl air-cooled radial
Power	1,147kW (1,538hp) each
Max speed	368kph
Range	1,900km
Ceiling	10,000m

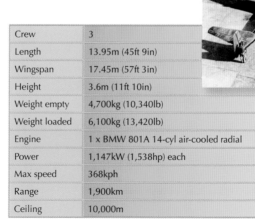

Blohm & Voss
BV 141.

GOODYEAR INFLATOPLANE

AN 'AIR' CRAFT IN MORE THAN ONE SENSE ... BUT DON'T FLY TOO CLOSE TO ROSE BUSHES

The idea behind the Goodyear Inflatoplane was simple, and basically quite sensible. An inflatable plane, just like a bouncy castle, could be stored in a relatively small container, and then inflated when needed.

The original concept of an all-fabric inflatable aircraft was based on inflatable glider experiments in 1931 by Taylor McDaniel. The first Goodyear Inflatoplane was designed and built in just twelve weeks in 1956, with the idea that it could be used by the military as a rescue plane to be dropped inside its hardened container behind enemy lines. It had a lot going for it. It could:

- Be transported in its container by lorry, jeep or aircraft.
- Take off from an airstrip just 250ft long, and after 575ft could clear a 50ft obstacle.
- Be inflated in just five minutes to 25psi, and could fly with inflation at just 8psi.
- Land in just 35ft.
- Climb to 10,000ft and achieve 72mph (116kph).
- Fly for six and a half hours on just 76 litres of fuel, over a range of 630km.

There were single- and two-seat variants, and later a more powerful 60hp was made available, but the range was reduced to 443km. The whole thing was kept rigid by constantly blowing air into it.

It sounded ideal for its specialised role. However, there were two slight snags. With fairly flexible wings, and a propeller mounted just above the wings, there was a risk of the wing flexing enough to get chopped to pieces. This happened, with fatal results, on one of the first test flights.

Secondly, the United States Army noticed a slight flaw in the whole concept, revealed by the simple statement when they cancelled the project: 'We could not find a valid military use for an aircraft that could be brought down by a well-aimed bow and arrow.'

Crew	1 (with no sharp buckles or long fingernails)
Length	5.8m (19ft 0in)
Wingspan	8.5m (27ft 11in)
Height	1.2m (3ft 11in)
Weight loaded	336kg (739lb)
Engine	1 x McCulloch 4318 air-cooled
Power	45kW (60hp)
Max speed	113kph
Range	440km
Altitude	1,981m
Armament	one puncture repair kit

Goodyear Inflatoplane.

CUSTER CCW-5

THE CUSTER'S LAST STAND?

There is a story, which may or may not be true, that the Trans-Siberian Railway is dead straight except for a strange kink in the middle of nowhere. The story is that the Tsar drew a straight line across Russia and ordered his railway engineers to build it. However, his thumb got in the way, producing the kink in the line. The engineers were so worried about disobeying the Tsar's orders that they included the kink in the actual railway line. Well, it makes a good story at least.

In the case of the Custer CCW-5 it looks like a similar thing happened when the wings were being designed.

Perhaps the chief designer had quickly sketched the new plane getting his thumb in the way when doing the wings … however, he managed the amazing feat of 'thumbing' it on both wings.

In reality the channel wings were designed to create incredible amounts of lift at very slow speeds. The Custer was capable of landing and taking off in less than 30m, and could land at a speed of just 24kph (15mph). It was claimed it could safely fly at just 18kph (11mph), although of what practical use that was escapes me.

Two were built, but the performance didn't quite match expectations. For example, the maximum speed was found to be 354kph rather than the hoped for 480kph. The one that still survives is being restored, and the only photographs show it in a sorry state in a hangar.

Crew	1
Passengers	4
Length	8.75m (28ft 8in)
Wingspan	12.55m (41ft 2in)
Height	3.30m (10ft 10in)
Weight empty	1,361kg (2,994lb)
Gross weight	2,449kg (5,388lb)
Engines	2 x Continental O-470-A flat-6 air-cooled
Power	168kW (225hp) each
Cruising speed	156kph
Max speed	354kph
Service ceiling	6,096m

Custer CCW-5.

JUNKERS G.38

DIESEL-POWERED LUXURY ... INSIDE THE WINGS!

The Junkers G.38 was the largest land plane in the world when it first appeared in 1929, and it was the pinnacle of luxury intended to rival that of the Zeppelin airships.

However, the luxury was not the most significant feature of these large aircraft. Several features made the G.38 unique at the time:

- When first flown most of the passengers actually sat inside the 1.7m thick wings, not in the fuselage. The leading edges of the wings were fitted with sloping windscreens giving passengers a panoramic view normally only enjoyed by pilots.

Crew	7
Length	23.21m (76ft 2in)
Wingspan	44.0m (144ft 4in)
Height	7.2m (23ft 7in)
Weight empty	14,920kg (32,824lb)
Weight loaded	24,000kg (52,800lb)
Engines	2 x Junkers Jumo L55 V12
	2 x Junkers Jumo L8a straight-6
Cruising speed	175kph
Max speed	225kph
Range	3,460km
Ceiling	3,690m

- Two passengers were accommodated right up in the nose, rather like bomb aimers.
- The G.38 was, almost uniquely, powered by diesel engines. There were four engines, two V12 and two straight-6 Junkers Jumo units, featuring a pair of opposed pistons in each cylinder.
- The crew were able to service the engines in flight from within the thick wings.
- When it first started service in 1931 on the Berlin-to-London route it had seven crew and just thirteen passenger seats, giving an unprecedented staff-to-passenger ratio.

Between 1929 and 1936 the engines increased in power output, and extra passenger accommodation was fitted, increasing the capacity to thirty.

In 1936 one of the two G.38s crashed during a post-maintenance test flight, but the pilot survived. The second G.38 completed almost a full decade of service with Lufthansa, and with the outbreak of war became a military transport. It was destroyed on the ground by the RAF in 1941. The design was also licensed to Mitsubishi who built six designated the Ki-20.

The photograph shows a G.38 at Schipol with, presumably, the people who had been on board. This particular plane was destroyed by the RAF in 1940 in Athens.

Junkers G.38.

ROCKWELL HiMAT

THE ULTIMATE COMPUTER GAME?

The Rockwell HiMAT (**Hi**ghly **Man**-oeuvrable **A**ircraft **T**echnology) was certainly a strange aircraft. Between 1979 and 1983 two of these were used by the NASA Dryden Flight Research Centre to develop high-performance fighter technologies that would subsequently be applied to later aircraft.

So why were they strange? They were actually flown from the comfort of an armchair on the ground. Having no pilot on board meant that the aircraft could be taken to extremes not possible in a manned craft. For example the HiMAT has been tested in 8G turns, whereas an F-16 with a human pilot can only achieve around 4.5G.

The HiMAT was launched from a B-52 bomber at around 12,000m altitude, and after the flight landed on the ground conventionally.

There is, however, one puzzle about the HiMAT. As it didn't carry a pilot, and was in any case too small to do so, why was it fitted with a cockpit cover?

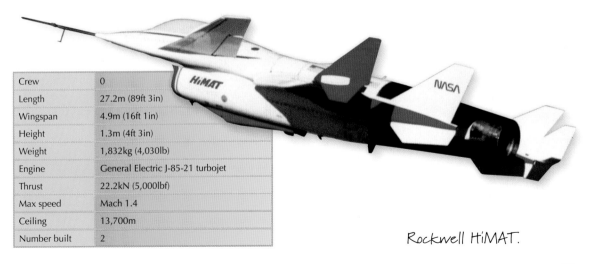

Crew	0
Length	27.2m (89ft 3in)
Wingspan	4.9m (16ft 1in)
Height	1.3m (4ft 3in)
Weight	1,832kg (4,030lb)
Engine	General Electric J-85-21 turbojet
Thrust	22.2kN (5,000lbf)
Max speed	Mach 1.4
Ceiling	13,700m
Number built	2

Rockwell HiMAT.

BOEING 747SP
(SURELY THIS IS A MISTAKE? ED.)

It is perfectly understandable that the reader might think including the 747 as 'strange', and in particular including it under the 'plane bonkers' category, must be a mistake, or that the author has spent too much time in the sun with just a few too many G&Ts (the latter may indeed be true). Surely the Boeing 747 is the most unstrange aircraft in the world today? Well, yes and no.

The 747 was conceived in the 1960s as air travel was increasing at a great rate. The 707s and DC-8s of the time were simply not large enough to move the number of people wishing to travel, and Pan Am asked Boeing to build an aircraft at least twice as large as the existing jet liners. In 1966 Pan Am ordered twenty-five of the new planes, named Boeing 747-100s, for a total of $525 million.

The recipe for success was simple. An aircraft that could carry up to 550 passengers, fly non-stop for around 6,000 miles, and deliver costs per passenger per mile at a record low level. Boeing had only ever expected

to make and sell around 400, but to date over 1,500 have been built in various configurations.

So how does the 747 qualify for being strange? Well, in 1976 some genius at Boeing decided there was

a role for a 'Special Performance' version, to be called the 747SP (originally it was to be called SB for 'Short Body', but later this was changed to the somewhat more ambiguous 'Special Performance').

Boeing 747SP.

The idea was to give super-long range and access to airports with short runways. There were just a few drawbacks to the idea:

- Reducing its length by 14m cut capacity from 550 to 331 passengers.
- The basic 747 design was only efficient when all 550 seats were full. The SP with only 331 seats cost virtually the same to operate, so the cost per passenger mile was over 60 per cent greater.
- The SP was designed for 'super-long-range' non-stop operation, but in practice its 'super-long range' ended up only around 9 per cent greater than the standard plane.
- The 'super performance' of the SP was shown off by performing round-the-world flights with just stops for refuelling, these lasting up to fifty-four hours. No one had asked whether any sane passenger would voluntarily sit in an aircraft for fifty-four hours without a break.
- The 'access to airports with short runways' turned out to be a red herring, as there were no airports with short runways requiring the capacity of the SP.
- By reducing the length of the 747 by 14m they turned an already non-too-attractive design into something which looked like it came from a kids' TV programme, and should have two eyes and a broad grinning smile on the front, and be called Jimmy the Jumbo.

So, yes, the idea was strange. Just forty-five were built between 1974 and 1989, and most of these were quickly fobbed off by the major airlines onto third-tier airlines in obscure countries wishing to jump on the 'Jumbo bandwagon' at any price. Just eighteen are still flying.

I rest my case. As a business concept it *was* 'plane bonkers'.

Cockpit Crew	3 (2 pilots + 1 engineer)
Seating capacity	331 (28 first, 303 economy)
Length	56.31m (184ft 9in)
Wingspan	59.64m (195ft 8in)
Height	20.06m (65ft 10in)
Weight empty	152,780kg (336,116lb)
Weight loaded	304,000kg (668,800lb)
Engines	4 x Pratt & Whitney JT7D or
	4 x Rolls-Royce RB211-524C2
Thrust x 4	206.8kN (46,490lbf)
Max speed	1,095kph (Mach 0.92)
Range	12,320km
Ceiling	13,750m
Fuel capacity	190,600 litres

CURTISS F9C SPARROWHAWK

YOU'D HAVE TO BE COMPLETELY BONKERS TO FLY THIS ONE

The Curtiss Sparrowhawk is not included here because the aircraft itself is bonkers. It's included because of the completely mad way it was designed to operate.

The airplane itself is quite sensible in fact, if rather on the small side. Just 6.1m (20ft) long and with a wingspan of 7.6m (25ft) it weighed a very modest 959kg (2,114lb) empty. The compact size and the very large hook above the upper wing are clues as to how it operated.

The Sparrowhawk was what is called a 'parasite fighter'. It was designed to be slung beneath an airship, and to

be released to attack enemy fighters should the airship come under attack. That was verging on being quite a good idea. However, the Sparrowhawk was intended to dock back under the airship by raising the large hook and attempting to hook onto what was called a 'flying trapeze'. In gusty conditions it could take several attempts to engage the hook. Once engaged the trapeze and the aircraft were raised inside the airship's hull.

As if that weren't bonkers enough, sometimes the Sparrowhawk would have its undercarriage removed to save weight and thereby increase its range. That meant that the poor pilot didn't even have the option of landing on the ground should the hooking up prove too difficult. Another novel use of the Sparrowhawk was as 'flying ballast'. The airship could take off with an extra load of fuel, and then later on when some of the fuel had been used the Sparrowhawk could fly up and latch on as new ballast.

In spite of the concept being completely madcap, seven were built and one survives.

Cockpit Crew	1
Length	6.27m (21.08ft)
Wingspan	7.75m (25.5ft)
Height	3.34m (10.9ft)
Weight empty	959kg (2,114lb)
Weight loaded	1,259kg (2,776lb)
Engine	1 x Wright R-975-E3
Power	310kW (415hp)
Max speed	283kph (176mph)
Range	475km (297 miles)
Ceiling	5,853m (19,200ft)
Armament	2 x 7.62mm Browning machine guns
Number built	7+

Curtiss F9C
Sparrowhawk.

DESIGNERS WITH LATENT WING FETISHES

Most aircraft designers today seem content to design aircraft with a single pair of wings, one on each side, together with smaller wings at the back as part of the tailplane. In the early days of aviation they often went as far as having two pairs of main wings, creating a biplane. Very occasionally we'd see a triplane with three pairs of wings. But up to three pairs of wings hardly rates as profligate 'winging'. However, some designers seem to have had some sort of weird wing fetish or addiction, and just didn't know how to, or didn't want to, stop adding wings. So we find the Caproni Ca.60 with nine pairs of wings, and the ultimate in 'wingsmanship', Horatio Phillips' Multiplane with no fewer than 200 small wings.

CAPRONI CA.60

WHY MAKE DO WITH JUST EIGHT PAIRS OF WINGS WHEN NINE WILL DO?

As far as I am aware, the Caproni Ca.60 is the only plane ever built with three sets of three wings each. I suppose technically it was a nono-plane. I can think of four possible explanations for the nine wings:

- Giovanni Battista Caproni, the Company's founder, had a rare aerofoil fetish.
- After a heavy night on the Grappa, Caproni fell over and banged his head, and suffered temporary double vision. Before full recovery he observed that birds with two pairs of wings flew faster than those with just one, and so deduced that a plane with nine wings should be exceptionally quick.

Crew	8 (sense of humour desirable)
Ideal IQ of pilot	<75
Capacity	100 passengers (brave)
Length	23.45m (76ft 11in)
Wingspan	30m (98ft 5in)
Height	9.15m (30ft 0in)
Weight loaded	26,000kg (57,200lb)
Engines	8 x Liberty L-12 V12 engines
Power	298kW (400hp) each
Cruising speed	130kph
Range	660km
Best feature	Lots of wings, in case one drops off
Worst feature	Wings very likely to drop off

Caproni Ca.60.

- Giovanni had been at the magic mushrooms again.
- His design team consisted of nine petulant young Italians who behaved like little children, and all wanted to design the wings. In a paternalistic gesture, Giovanni agreed that each of the nine could do one wing each, provided they were all roughly the same length.

The nine wings made it so top heavy it had to be equipped with two large pontoon outriggers to keep it stable on water. Also it was almost completely symmetrical lengthwise, which must have caused a little confusion prior to take-off.

It was built as a prototype flying boat to carry 100 passengers across the Atlantic, although its range of just 600 miles might have posed a few operational problems in that role. It would have required five filling stations to be anchored in the ocean. Only one Ca.60 was built, and this made just a single flight from Lake Maggiore when it attained the dizzy height of 18m before crashing. The pilot was unscathed. The aircraft, however, was very scathed, and the wreck was towed ashore. Caproni announced he would rebuild it. However, that very night it burned to ashes. I suspect his psychiatrist might have had a role to play in this ... and if he didn't have a psychiatrist then I think he should have had one.

There is a good-quality photograph of the aircraft being built. The photograph is interesting in that there is only one person in it. Maybe it's Caproni himself. Maybe the whole thing was a one-man DIY project. Indeed he might have had problems persuading anyone else to devote their time to such a daft venture.

Caproni Ca.60 under construction.

THE FLYING VENETIAN BLIND

Horatio Phillips' Multiplanes possibly set the gold standard as the most bizarre creations ever to fly. Horatio Phillips was born in 1845 in Streatham, and was one of the earliest aviation pioneers in the UK. He experimented with lifting surfaces, and devised a wind tunnel, which was unusual in that the gas flow was provided by steam rather than air. It is just possible this explains his wacky designs. Maybe his glasses kept getting steamed up, and the clouds of steam in the wind tunnel prevented him from seeing just how way out his designs really were. Or maybe he was simply a nutcase.

Phillips believed that multiple stacked wings, which he called 'sustainers', offered advantages over normal wings. His first flying machine in 1893 had fifty wings. It did fly, but not carrying a person.

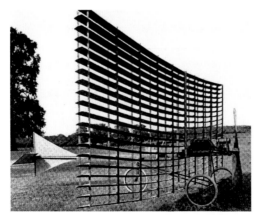

Horatio Phillips' plane.

Horatio Phillips' Multiplane.

He used it to test lifting ability, and the modest fifty-winger was able to lift 400lb.

His next Multiplane in 1904 had just twenty-one wings but added a tail for stability. It was designed to carry a pilot but proved incapable of sustained flight, the best attempt being one of just 50ft. I cannot think what was going through Phillips' mind when he imagined a mere twenty-one wings would carry a man. However, I do suspect where he got inspiration from. One photograph shows his 1904 Multiplane, and the other a venetian blind mounted on a tricycle. I can't help but think that the venetian blind on a tricycle looks marginally the more sensible device.

Realising the weakness of a serious lack of wings, Phillips' next creation in 1907 had no fewer than 200 individual 'winglets'. With its 22hp engine and a 7ft propeller, it managed a flight of 500ft. Actually this was, at the time, a record for a flight in the UK, and probably remains to this day a record for a flying venetian blind. However, the 1907 version showed poor performance compared to more conventional designs, and Phillips gave up manned flight to concentrate on more technical aspects of aviation. The third photograph is a contemporary one of his 1907 machine. Unfortunately, no better photographs seem to have survived.

Had his ideas been more successful, and caught on, I do wonder what the modern Boeing 747-400 or Airbus A380 might look like. Maybe they'd have 400 and 380 wings respectively!

Horatio Phillips' plane.

MCDONNELL DOUGLAS X-36

THE WORLD'S FIRST TWO-DIMENSIONAL AIRCRAFT?

The McDonnell Douglas X-36 'Tailless Fighter Agility Research Aircraft', first flown in 1997, was a scaled-down version of an aircraft designed to fly without a traditional tail. It was a 28 per cent scale version of a potential fighter aircraft, and as it was so small it was in fact flown remotely from the ground.

Its two main physical characteristics are, as the name suggests, the absence of any tailplane, and a pair of canard wings, which unusually are almost as large as the main wings.

There are various explanations as to why the X-36 ended up essentially two-dimensional:

Crew	0
Length	5.56m (18ft 3in)
Wingspan	3.15m (10ft 4in)
Height	0.95m (3ft 1in)
Weight loaded	560kg (1,232lb)
Engine	1 x Williams International F112 turbofan
Power	3.1kN (697lbf)
Max speed	375kph
Ceiling	6,100m
Best feature	It's piloted from the ground
Worst feature	It's difficult to tell which way up it is
Number built	2

- The design team sat in two separate rooms, and someone lost the key to the connecting door so that models of the design had to be squeezed through the narrow gap under the door.
- The chief designer has a rare tailplane allergy.
- The tail was left until Friday afternoon to be designed, but the whole team bunked off early to the pub.
- They simply ran out of metal.

The unusual design resulted in a plane that was highly unstable, didn't like flying in a straight line (tails do help there) but equally got the jitters when thoughts like 'turn' entered the remote pilot's brain. A highly complex 'fly by wire' computer system was required at vast expense to keep the thing flying straight … when a couple of hundred dollars of tail metal would have done the job just as well, if not better. With this complex computer control it was said to 'handle very well' and 'exceeded all project goals', which maybe is why the programme was promptly axed after just thirty-one flights.

McDonnell Douglas X-36.

PROTEUS

A TRUE AVIATION HIGH-FLYER

At a quick glance through half-closed eyes, Proteus looks like three separate craft flying in dangerously close formation. But the whole thing is one delicate skeleton designed to fly at almost impossible altitudes for unbelievable lengths of time. Technically it is called a tandem-wing high-endurance aircraft, and is another design

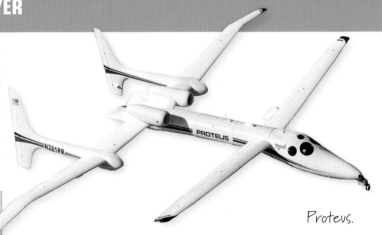

Proteus.

Crew	2 (pilot and co-pilot)
Length	17.17m (56ft 4in)
Wingspan	23.65m (77ft 7in)
Height	5.38m (17ft 8in)
Weight empty	2,658kg (5,848lb)
Max weight	5,670kg (12,474lb)
Engines	2 x Williams FJ44-2 turbofans
Power	10.20kN (2,293lbf) each
Cruising speed	352kph
Max speed	504kph
Endurance	14 hours
Service ceiling	18,593m
Armament	none
Number built	1

from Burt Rutan, some of whose craft have already been covered in this book.

Proteus includes an all composite airframe with graphite/epoxy sandwich construction, making it very light. The wingspan may be increased from 23.65m to 28m with the unique addition of removable wing tips. Another unique feature is that it may either be piloted, or controlled remotely without a pilot from the ground. One of its main applications is as a mobile communications platform for use where ordinary radio signals are weak.

Proteus holds a number of Fédération Aéronautique Internationale (FAI) world records for altitude, the highest altitude achieved being 19,277m (63,245ft), which puts it close to the edge of space. With this capability Proteus has been used in a very wide variety of roles.

OERTZ W6 FLUGSCHONER

THE FLYING SCHOONER

Max Oertz's aircraft were simply boats with wings attached. This was not really surprising since Oertz was originally a boat builder. The Flying Schooner was unusual in having tandem wings mounted above the hull with a pair of pusher propellers placed between the pairs of wings, each powered by a Maybach engine. The engines were hidden inside the hull, and drove the propellers via chains.

At first Oertz only put ailerons on the forward set of wings, which, with the pusher propellers placed between the two sets, did little for controllability. So a second set was quickly added on the rear wings.

The whole design resulted in massive drag, both from the hull and the two sets of wings, and speed was seriously compromised. However, although it would have been totally useless in combat, the German Navy found it useful for reconnaissance and several were built.

Crew	?
Length	14.53m (47ft 8in)
Wingspan	20.0m (65ft 7in)
Wing area	162.7m²
Height	4.78m (15ft 8in)
Weight empty	3,780kg (8,316lb)
Gross weight	5,030kg (11,066lb)
Engines	2 x Maybach Mb IV
Power	179kW (240hp) each
Max speed	115–118kph
Number built	possibly 10

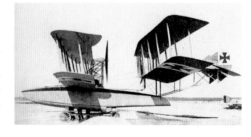

Oertz W6 Flugschoner.

BOEING B-29 'TIP TOW'
AIRBORNE SIAMESE TRIPLETS!

The photograph of the B-29 'Tip Tow' looks like a clever bit of Photoshop work, but it was real.

In reality 'Tip Tow' was a cunning plan to extend the range of jet fighters by having them piggyback, or in the case of the B-29, 'piggyside' until they got closer to their intended targets. Amazingly the pilots of the two fighter 'children' maintained control of their aircraft whilst attached, the link being a hinge rather than a rigid connection. The engines of the two F-84s were, however, shut down to save fuel.

Crew	13
Length	30.18m (99ft 0in)
Wingspan	65.26m (214ft 1in)
Weight empty	44,200kg (97,440lb)
Weight loaded	70,400kg (156,160lb)
Engines	2 x Allison J35 turbjets
	4 x Wright R3350 turbo-charged radial
Power	49.4kN (11,120lb) ... plus
	... 6,560kW (8,800hp)
Cruising speed	350kph (220mph)
Max speed	574kph (357mph)
Range	B29: 5,230km (3,250 miles) F84: 1,600km (1,000 miles)

However, the fighters were not attached on take-off, as this would have been far too tricky and dangerous. Instead the fighters took off separately and then locked onto a boom extended from the B-29's wing tips. Once engaged the boom retracted to lock all three craft together. Apparently this manoeuvre, although successful in practice, was challenging because of heavy turbulence caused by the B-29's wings.

Unfortunately the exercise ended in disaster. In order to make the whole operation 'safer' the control of the two fighters was made automatic, controlled from the 'mother' plane. On the very first test flight the left-hand F-84 rolled onto the wing of the B-29 and all three aircraft crashed to the ground with no survivors.

Surprisingly this did not end the programme. Three years later the same technique was revived, but this time using modified F-84s and the massive B-36 Peacemaker. After fifty successful hook-ups tragedy nearly struck again, when one of the F-84s became unstable after link-up. However, on this occasion both fighters managed to disengage and all three aircraft landed safely. The programme was stopped shortly afterwards on safety grounds.

The statistics in the Fact Box refer to the complete three-plane setup.

Boeing B-29 'Tip Tow'.

ZERBE SEXTUPLANE

A SIX-WINGED ONE-DAY WONDER

The Sextuplane was a highly unconventional aircraft built in 1919 by Professor Jerome Slough Zerbe. It had six heavily staggered wings mounted above a framework in which the pilot and engine were located. Propulsion was by a single tractor propeller. The Sextuplane was a development of the Zerbe Quintaplane, which of course had just five wings. The Quintaplane had not been a success, its only attempted flight being in 1910 in Los Angeles, in which it hit a pothole when attempting to take off and fell to pieces.

Known also as the Zerbe Air Sedan, the only record of it actually flying was at the Washington County Fairground where it is said the pilot, Tom Flannerty, flew it for around 1,000ft, attaining an altitude of 40 or 50ft, although some reports claim it was 40–50in!

Zerbe was not a great success as an aircraft designer and he disappeared from all historical records around 1920. Maybe no bad thing, as I cannot imagine what his design ideas might have done for Concorde or the Boeing 747.

Zerbe Sextuplane.

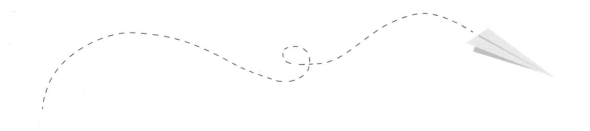

IS DOUBLE VISION A COMMON PROBLEM IN THE AERONAUTICAL DESIGN OFFICE?

We've all been there at some time. A really heavy night out, and somehow the two eyes that God kindly gave us don't seem too keen on working in harmony. Or, in the case of the much less fortunate, a nasty bump on the head can induce what we might call dual images. It appears that aircraft designers are not immune from these misfortunes, and we end up with aircraft that seem to duplicate rather basic elements of the design like the fuselage.

There again, maybe the problem isn't double vision at all, but early-onset Alzheimer's. Could it be that the designer did design the fuselage on the Tuesday, but on returning to work on the Wednesday forgot he (or she) had done it, and so designed it a second time.

Anyway, whatever the cause, we do find quite a lot of aircraft that manifest the physical consequences of UADDS (Unexplained Aircraft Design Duality Syndrome).

NORTH AMERICAN XF-82 TWIN MUSTANG

WAS THIS THE RESULT OF TWO TEST PILOTS BEHAVING LIKE SPOILT CHILDREN?

One possible explanation for the design of the North American Twin Mustang is that there were two equally senior test pilots, and they bickered so much like little children that in the end the chief designer decided to give them both a cockpit. I do hope only one had full control, though (no, actually both did!).

The reality, however, is less interesting. The XF-82 was intended as a very-long-range escort fighter to fly with the Boeing B-29 Superfortress on missions of over 3,200km (2,000 miles) from the Philippines to Japan. This distance was beyond the range of the existing P-51 Mustangs and Lockheed P-38 Lightnings. These missions were planned as part of the proposed invasion of Japan. However, the atom bombs dropped at Hiroshima and Nagasaki led to the Japanese surrender, so the invasion became unnecessary.

To give the extra range the basic fuselage of the P-51 Mustang was lengthened to provide more space for fuel tanks, and the two fuselages on the Twin Mustang were connected by a central wing section, which also contained fuel in addition to the six 12.7mm Browning machine guns.

The original plan had been to use Packard-built Rolls-Royce Merlin V12 engines, with the propellers rotating in opposite directions to make take-off and landing more stable, there then being no net gyroscopic force from the propellers. Initially there was a serious design fault: the propellers were designed so that the blades were turning upwards

Crew	2
Length	12.93m (42ft 9in)
Wingspan	15.62m (51ft 3in)
Wing area	37.9m² (408ft²)
Height	4.22m (13ft 10in)
Weight empty	7,271kg (15,997lb)
Gross weight	11,632kg (25,591lb)
Engines	2 x Allison V-1710-143/145 V12
Power	1,029kW (1,380hp) each
Max speed	740kph (482mph)
Range	3,605km (2,350 miles)
Armament	6 x 12.7mm Browning M3 machine guns
	25 x 127mm rockets
	1,800kg (4,000lb) bombs
Number built	270

when they passed the central wing, but this arrangement was found to create enough drag to cancel out all the lift generated by the central wing section, with the result that the Twin Mustang refused to leave the ground. The propeller rotation was reversed and the problem was solved. However, for various political and cost reasons the engines were changed from Rolls-Royce Merlins to Allison V-1710-100s. The Twin Mustang was designed with full controls in both cockpits, so that on long flights the two pilots could take turns. I assume bickering between the two pilots was not a problem.

As it turned out the Twin Mustang saw no action in the Second World War. Although some airframes were completed by 1945, none was flown until 1946 as there was a delay in the delivery of the Allison engines. In fact the Allison engines gave inferior performance compared to the early Merlin-powered prototypes.

The Twin Mustang, which was the very last propeller-driven fighter

North American XP-82 Twin Mustang.

used by the US Air Force, still holds a world record. In February 1947 a P-82B flew non-stop from Hawaii to New York, a distance of 8,129km (5,051 miles) in fourteen hours and thirty-two minutes at an average speed of 559.2kph (347.5mph). This remains to this day the longest non-stop flight made by a propeller-driven

fighter, and the fastest such a distance has ever been covered by a piston-engined aircraft. Interestingly, and rather pleasing for Rolls-Royce, this was one of the early Merlin-powered examples.

THIS MUST BE ONE OF THE UGLIEST AIRCRAFT EVER MADE.

In the case of the Twin Mustang, double vision in the drawing office resulted in something really quite elegant. In the case of the Savoia-Marchetti S.55P it resulted in something really quite exceptionally hideous.

However, to be fair, whilst it certainly was hideously ugly it was amazingly successful, setting no less than fourteen world records for speed, payload, altitude and range, and over 243 were made. The aircraft had two hulls, which also formed the floats, and all the passengers were located in these hulls. The crew, however, sat in a cockpit located in the thick middle-wing section. The S.55P had two engines, sitting back to back and located very high up, and driving contra-rotating propellers. The triple-finned tail structure was attached to the twin hulls and wings by wire-braced booms.

Most notable of the aircraft's achievements were the flights across the Atlantic. In particular, in 1933, a flight of twenty-four S.55Ps flew in a tight 'V' formation from Orbetello in Italy to Chicago for the Century of Progress Exposition in just over forty-eight hours. It would also find a role as a bomber, but by the Second World War none was serviceable and none saw any action. One S.55P survives as a non-flying exhibit in Brazil.

Crew	5–6
Length	16.75m (55ft 0in)
Wingspan	24.0m (74ft 9in)
Wing area	93m² (1,001ft²)
Height	5.0m (16ft 5in)
Weight empty	5,750kg (12,677lb)
Engines	2 x Isotta Fraschini Asso 750V
Power	656kW (880hp) each
Max speed	279kph (173mph)
Range	3,500km (2,200 miles)
Armament	4 x 7.7mm machine guns
	1 x torpedo or
	2,000kg (4,409lb) bombs
Number built	270

Savoia-Marchetti S.55P.

NORTHROP XP-79B

WAS IT MODELLED ON A STINGRAY?

At first glance, the Northrop XP-79B appears to manifest not only symptoms of double vision, but also symptoms of early-onset Alzheimer's. It looks as though the designer forgot one rather important feature, that of a cockpit. But in fact, within the large void between the air intakes, the pilot lay prone in a coffin like 'cockpit', in which position it was believed he could withstand much greater G-forces than if sat upright.

The XP-79B's development was what is known technically in the aircraft design world as 'a complete cock-up'. Originally the plan had been to use an Aerojet XCALR-2000A-1 rocket motor, which used as fuel mono-ethyl aniline and fuming nitric acid. Because of the savage corrosive nature of fuming nitric acid the aircraft was built, not of riveted aluminium, but of welded magnesium alloy. Now, as every schoolchild knows, magnesium is just a little tricky to work with, and welding a magnesium alloy is about as easy as trying to eat an ice cream whilst sitting in the exhaust duct of a Rolls-Royce Trent turbofan on full throttle. However, the rocket power solution was found wanting, and instead two Westinghouse 19-B (J30) turbojets were used instead. This meant that the ridiculously expensive and difficult welded-magnesium construction was no longer needed, but it was still used.

The test programme was equally disastrous. After long delays because of tyres bursting and braking problems, the single prototype XP-79 finally took off on 12 September 1945 and promptly crashed. The pilot bailed out but was then struck by the aircraft and fell to his death. The programme was then cancelled.

Crew	1
Length	4.27m (14ft 0in)
Wingspan	11.58m (38ft 0in)
Wing area	25.8m² (278ft²)
Height	2.29m (7ft 6in)
Weight empty	2,650kg (5,840lb)
Engines	2 x Westinghouse 19-B turbojet
Power	5.1kN (1,150lbf) each
Max speed	880kph (547mph)
Range	1,598km (993 miles)
Armament	4 x 12.7mm machine guns (never fitted)
Number built	1

Northrop XP-79B.

VMS EVE WHITE KNIGHT

DOUBLE VISION IS STILL A PROBLEM IN DESIGN OFFICES

Apart from being the latest double-fuselage aircraft, the VMS Eve White Knight is unique in a number of ways. Built by Scaled Composites for the Virgin Group, it is the largest all-composite aircraft ever built, and also has the longest single-piece composite aircraft component of all time with its 43m (140ft) wingspan, constructed as one piece. The composite construction makes it very light and fuel efficient, indeed the most fuel-efficient plane of its size ever.

Its other unique feature is that it was built as the launch platform both for Virgin Galactic and for the Virgin Spaceships, the first time an aircraft will have been used in this way. The photograph shows White Knight with the SpaceShipTwo attached underneath between the two fuselages.

The White Knight has exceptional lifting power, being able to carry a payload of 16,000kg (35,000lb) up to an altitude of 15,300m (50,000ft).

Crew	2 + spaceship launch crew
Capacity	payload 17,000kg (37,000lb) to 15,000m
Length	24m (78.75ft)
Wingspan	43m (141ft 1in)
Engines	4 x Pratt & Whitney Canada PW308 turbofan
Power	30.69kN (6,900lbf) each
Ceiling	21,000m (70,000ft)
Number built	1 (one more possible)

VMS Eve White Knight.

AIRCRAFT DESIGNED BY A KIDDIES' ORIGAMI CLASS

Some aircraft leave you with a clear impression they were actually designed in a kindergarten origami session. I can see the scenario clearly. The designer has frittered away the day in the design office buying and selling things on eBay, organising next Saturday's darts match, checking comparison websites for his car insurance, and chatting on Facebook – a typical office day – and when he is about to leave promptly at 4.45 p.m. to pick up his daughter from playschool, the chief designer walks in and asks how the design for the new aircraft is developing, and tells him that the client will be in at 8.30 sharp the next morning to approve the drawings.

Panic sets in. He cannot delay at the office otherwise he'll be locked away for five years for child neglect, so he rushes out to the kindergarten. But salvation is at hand. On entering the kindergarten his delightful 3-year-old thrusts a paper aeroplane into his hand with the exclamation 'Daddy, look what I made today!'

In that instant the design for the new European Multi-Role Super-Mega-Doom-Star Fighter/Bomber was conceived. Even better, the designer had, with the addition of some felt-tip pen work later that evening, a scaled-down mock-up to show the European military bigwigs in the morning.

The following morning comments like 'That's brilliant! It looks just like it could have been conceived in a kindergarten origami class', and 'It's even better than the US stealth bomber ... I think that one WAS designed by a kiddies' origami class' could be heard in the board room. Great news for the designer ... and so, off the hook, and yet another day buying and selling on eBay and following Facebook.

HYPER 111

It would be extremely challenging to design an aircraft that looks more like a folded sheet of A4 paper than the Hyper 111. But although it looks just like a paper dart, the Hyper 111 was a real aircraft, albeit a remotely piloted one.

The Hyper 111 was designed to help research in the M2 lifting body programme. It had no engine and no control surfaces on the wings. It was equipped with twin tail fins and rudders at a 40° angle, and hinged 'elevons' on the flat part of the body. The landing gear was a fixed tricycle arrangement, and it had an emergency parachute system. Control was through a five-channel radio link, and instrument data was downloaded via a twelve-channel link.

Crew	0
Length	9.75m (32ft)
Wingspan	4.57m (15ft)
Wing area	3.29m^2 (35.4ft^2)
Height	2.29m (7.5ft)
Weight empty	431kg (950lb)
Gross weight	431kg (950lb)
Engine	none
Power	0kN (0lbf)
Max speed	277kph (173ph)
Stall speed	111kph (69mph)
Range	18km (11 miles)
Ceiling	3,660m (12,000ft)
Number built	1

Hyper 111.

It made its one and only flight on 12 December 1969, when it was launched from a helicopter at 10,000ft. It glided for 5km, turned round and came back, and landed successfully. After an airborne career lasting just three minutes it never flew again as NASA cancelled the programme.

NORTHROP TACIT BLUE

IS IT POSSIBLE FOR AN AIRCRAFT TO BE ANY MORE 'SQUARE'?

In 1996, fourteen years after it was built, a very senior engineer at Northrop was quoted as saying: 'You're talking about an aircraft that at the time was arguably the most unstable aircraft man has ever flown.' On first glance it seems a miracle the Tacit Blue ever flew at all, stable or unstable. At the time it earned the nicknames of 'the whale' and 'the alien school bus', for obvious reasons.

The Tacit Blue was described at the time as a 'stealth demonstrator'. The basic idea seemed to be that a very low-flying stealth surveillance aircraft could fly forward to the front lines of a conflict with a very low probability of being detected by radar. I do suspect that another advantage would be that any enemy seeing the Tacit Blue flying low overhead might well die laughing before having a chance to contact HQ.

A single flush inlet on the top of the fuselage, visible in the photograph above the conservatory, sorry cockpit, provided air to two high-bypass turbofans. As the engineer quoted earlier said the Tacit Blue was virtually uncontrollable, and the aircraft employed a quadruply redundant digital fly-by-wire flight-control system to stabilise the airborne bronco.

Somehow it flew, and over a three-year period over 135 test flights were completed. It was then retired and is now on display at the US Air Force's National Museum.

Crew	1
Length	17m (55ft 10in)
Wingspan	14.7m (48ft 2in)
Height	3.2m (10ft 7in)
Gross weight	13,606kg (30,000lb)
Engines	2 x Garrett ATF3-6 high-bypass turbofans
Power	24kN (5,440lbf) each
Max speed	462kph (287mph)
Ceiling	9,150m (30,000ft)
Number built	1

Northrop Tacit Blue.

BOEING X-32

THE ORIGAMI CLASS ONLY DESIGNED THE LOWER HALF

The X-32 has a somewhat schizophrenic appearance, as if the upper half were designed by engineers but when it got time to go home and the design wasn't finished the lower half design was handed to the local kindergarten's origami club. This has given it a rather pregnant frog-like appearance. From the waist up it looks like a normal fighter aircraft; from the waist down it resembles a couple of rubbish skips lashed together. The X-32 was a concept demonstrator in the Joint Strike Fighter contest in the United States, losing out in the end to the Lockheed Martin X-35 which was further developed into the F-35 Lightning II. It may be ungenerous to suggest that the Lockheed Martin design won simply because it didn't resemble a singing pregnant bullfrog.

In fact the story is somewhat more complicated. The Common Affordable Lightweight Fighter project (CALF) called for a single stealth-enabled design to replace the F-16 Falcon, the McDonnell Douglas F/A-18 Hornet, and the V/STOL Harrier. So the X-32 had to be capable of both supersonic speed and vertical take-off. The pregnant bullfrog appearance was the result of having a single, large centrally located thrust-vectoring nozzle for the V/STOL role. The large 'chin' at the front was necessary to allow the F-32 to take on the enormous volumes of air required whilst hovering, when there would be no 'ram effect' from forward movement.

Unfortunately there was a slight problem. Because of the heavy delta-wing design on the prototypes, Boeing found they couldn't demonstrate the supersonic and V/STOL capabilities on the same aircraft, and so used two different ones with a promise that when it came to production one design would achieve both objectives.

But Boeing lost the competition to Lockheed Martin, and work on the X-32 was stopped.

Crew	1
Length	13.72m (45.01ft)
Wingspan	10.97ms (36ft)
Weight loaded	17,200kg (38,000lb)
Engine	1 x Pratt & Whitney F119 turbofan
Dry thrust	125kN (28,000lbf)
With afterburner	191kN (43,000lbf)
Max speed	1,931kph (1,200mph)
Range	1,574km (850 miles)
Armament	20mm M61A2 cannon or
	27mm Mauser BK-27 cannon
	6,800kg external load (bombs/rockets)
Number built	1

Boeing X-32.

NASA X-43 SCRAMJET

IS THIS THE ULTIMATE AIRBORNE ORIGAMI?

The experimental X-43 took the origami look to extremes. It looks like little more than a sheet of paper with a couple of folds at the rear and a lump of Blu-Tack underneath. But this simple, almost naive, appearance conceals something extraordinary. Firstly it is the fastest plane that has ever flown, achieving 10,617kph (6,598mph) in November 2004. Secondly, when it is flying at top speed it has no moving parts in the engine. This calls for a little explanation.

A scramjet is, basically, just a tube with air flowing in at one end, fuel being injected in the middle, and a much greater blast of air going out at the back – simple, and no moving parts.

There is a slight problem, though. Scramjets don't work below around Mach 4.5, which in the technical language of the aeronautical engineer is ******* fast. To get to this speed the NASA X-43 is first launched from below a B-52 bomber at around 400mph. Then a rocket on board the

craft is fired taking it to the critical Mach 4.5, whereupon the scramjet is fired, taking it to Mach 7 – that is seven times the speed of sound. Later versions of the X-43 were designed to reach Mach 9.8, or 11,000kph (6,600mph). At this speed a flight from Heathrow to JFK would take thirty-one minutes. However, in practice the scramjet on the X-43 was designed to run for just eleven seconds, during which it covered 24km (15 miles). At the end of the flight the X-43 was designed to free-fall into the Pacific Ocean. So not only is it aeronautical origami, it is disposable aeronautical origami.

The X-43 was superseded by the X-43B, which had an even more complicated launch routine, involving the B-52, then a jet turbine, then a rocket, then a ramjet taking over at Mach 2.5 and finally the scramjet finishing the job from Mach 5 up to Mach 10 or more. Finally as part of this programme the X-43D was planned to be built to reach Mach 15, cutting the Heathrow to JFK time to twenty minutes.

In 2006 the Air Force Research Laboratory decided the X-43 was simply too tame, and the programme was stopped, to be superseded by the more ambitious X-51.

NASA X-43 Scramjet.

WHAT HAPPENS WHEN AIRCRAFT DESIGNERS WEAR THE WRONG SPECTACLES

It comes to us all in time … the day when we can no longer blame poor light or shrinking text size for the fact we can't read anything. And so we join the ranks of the reading glasses wearers. Then we come to rely on the reading glasses more and more, and the day we forget them we're sunk. Everyone of a 'certain age' will fully relate to this problem. For those not of a 'certain age' it will come, and sooner than you expect!

In the case of some aircraft, I can only assume it was a form of ocular mishap which spawned the aeronautic offspring (should that be abortions?) shown here. Maybe the designer picked up someone else's reading glasses, or simply tried to do without any at all, and started confusing wings with engines, landing gear with tailplane, or misread 'design a single-engine bomber' as 'design a silly English boathouse'. Simple mistakes, easily made.

GRANVILLE BROTHERS GEE BEE R-2 SUPER SPORTSTER

WAS THIS INSPIRED BY A DUSTBIN?

The Gee Bee R-2 was a purpose-built racing aircraft built by the Granville Brothers. Looking at its appearance I suspect it stood a good chance of winning races by the simple expedient of scaring the other competitors to death.

Looking at the design a number of things become evident:

- On a critical day in the design phase the Granville Brothers mislaid their spectacles (and, some may add, their brains!).
- It was inspired by a dustbin.
- The designer at first forgot it needed a cockpit, and quickly tagged one on just in front of the tail as an afterthought.

First flight	1932
Crew	1
Length	5.38m (17ft 8in)
Wingspan	7.62m (25ft 4in)
Height	2.48m (8ft 2in)
Weight empty	834kg (1,835lb)
Weight loaded	1095kg (2,409lb)
Engine	1 x Pratt & Whitney R-1340 Wasp 9-cyl radial
Power	596.5kW (800hp)
Max speed	473.8kph
Stall speed	144kph
Range	1,488km

- Given the position of the cockpit, take-offs would be totally blind.

Actually, if you hold the book at quite an acute angle, and half close your eyes, it starts to look less like a dustbin and more (well, not a lot more) like an aircraft.

To be fair to the Gee Bee, however, it did have quite a distinguished career. It won the 1932 Thompson Trophy piloted by Jimmy Doolittle, and also held the world landplane speed record at 476kph. However, it proved to be a very dangerous and difficult plane to fly, being basically just a Pratt & Whitney engine with wings attached. It had a very low polar moment of inertia and tiny control surfaces, making an aircraft that could easily get the better of all but the most experienced pilots. It crashed three times, being rebuilt on the first two occasions. However, the third crash, which killed the pilot, saw the end of the Gee Bee.

Granville Brothers Gee Bee.

COLOMBAN CRI-CRI

THE SMALLEST TWIN-ENGINE AIRCRAFT EVER BUILT

The Cri-Cri (the French words for the sound a cricket makes) is quite simply the smallest twin-engined aircraft the world has ever seen. Whether this was by design, or whether the creator, Frenchman Michel Colomban, was wearing the wrong spectacles is not known.

Designed in the early 1970s, the Cri-Cri without doubt scores very highly on the 'cuteness' scale, albeit at the expense of making the pilot appear as though he is sitting in a fish bowl. Amazingly the Cri-Cri is capable of aerobatics, provided the pilot is brave enough.

Colomban Cri-Cri.

Crew	1
Length	3.9m (12ft 10in)
Wingspan	4.9m (16ft 1in)
Weight empty	78kg (172lb)
Weight loaded	170kg (375lb)
Engines	2 x JPX PUL 212 single-cylinder
Power	11kw (15hp) each
Max speed	220kph (137mph)
Range	463km (288 miles)
Ceiling	3,700m (12,139ft)

The concept was taken one step further in 2010 when a four-engined electric version was produced, making it by far the smallest four-engine aircraft ever. It was capable of flying for thirty minutes at 110kph. A second electric Cri-Cri with twin motors set a world record for a lithium-battery-powered plane by achieving 262kph (162.33mph).

CAPRONI STIPA

WAS THIS A UNIQUE CARNIVOROUS AIRCRAFT?

Most people's reaction on seeing the photograph of the Caproni Stipa is to burst into uncontrollable laughter so intense as to threaten muscular injury to the chest. On first glance it looks like a carnivorous aircraft that has just swallowed whole a de Havilland Chipmunk. It is certainly testament to the fact that some aircraft designers have a sense of humour.

The Caproni Stipa, also rather confusingly known as the Stipa Caproni, was the brain-orphan of Luigi Stipa, and it was built by Caproni. It was basically an enormous barrel containing an engine and propeller. So in essence it was a ducted fan, very much like a modern turbofan engine. Indeed it has been said that Stipa's 'intubed propeller' design, with the engine inside a venturi tube, was the original inspiration for the fan jet. It might also have inspired the inventor of the Flymo lawnmower, of course.

Possibly unique amongst all aircraft ever built, its total length is less than twice its height. Pilots certainly needed to have a head for heights to even get inside the thing. The Caproni Stipa developed exceptional lift even at low speeds, and the landing speed of just 68kph was amazing. In addition, all test pilots reported that it was incredibly stable, so stable in fact that sometimes it became difficult to even change direction, not ideal of course.

Eventually the Caproni Stipa failed to show significant advantages over more conventional designs, and development work ceased.

First flight	1932
Crew	1 or 2
Length	5.88m (19ft 3in)
Wingspan	14.28m (46ft 10in)
Height	3m (9ft 10in)
Weight loaded	800kg (1,760lb)
Engine	1 x de Havilland Gipsy III inline piston engine
Power	90kW
Max speed	131kph
Landing speed	68kph
Number built	1

Caproni Stipa.

PZL-MIELEC M-18A DROMADER

IT LOOKS ODD FOR A VERY GOOD REASON

Crew	1
Capacity	one passenger + 2,500 litres or 2,200kg
Length	9.47m (31ft 1in)
Wingspan	17.7m (58ft)
Height	3.70m (12ft 1in)
Weight empty	2,710kg (5,975lb)
Weight loaded	5,300kg (11,700lb)
Engine	1 x WSK PZL-Kalisz ASz-621R radial
Power	731kW (980hp)
Max speed	230kph (143mph)
Stall speed	108kph (68mph)
Range	970km (602 miles)
Ceiling	6,500m (21,320ft)

It's really a little unfair to include this Polish aircraft here. It may look a little strange, but that appearance is for a very good reason. The cockpit is perched very high up in the middle of the plane not because the designer was wearing distorting glasses, but because the Dromader is basically an engine strapped to an enormous tank with a pilot sitting on top.

The Dromader is one of the world's most successful and widely used crop-dusting and firefighting aircraft, with over 760 manufactured since its first flight in 1976. Strange in some ways maybe, but strange in the best possible way.

PZL-Mielec
M-18A Dromader.

TRANSAVIA PL-12 AIRTRUK

IS THIS THE CUTEST THING THAT EVER FLEW?

If ever an aircraft should have two big eyes and a smiling face, and be called Colin, it's definitely the Transavia PL-12 Airtruk.

The Airtruk is a single-seat agricultural aircraft built by the Transavia Corporation in Australia. It was developed from the Bennett Airtruk designed by Luigi Pellarini in New Zealand, which had been built originally from bits of war-surplus North American Harvards. The Airtruk managed to avoid the Harvard parts bin, and whereas the Bennett plane had been pig ugly, the Airtruk ended up most attractive and amazingly cute.

The cockpit is mounted directly above the engine, giving excellent visibility for crop spraying, and behind the engine and cockpit is a 1-metric-tonne hopper. Alternatively the hopper space can be used for passengers, making the Airtruk the world's shortest and smallest two-deck aircraft, carrying one passenger 'upstairs' and four more 'downstairs'. It is also very unusual in having two tail booms that are not connected.

It's probably unfair to include it here as 'strange', but it is unusual for an aircraft to look like something from children's daytime TV.

Crew	1
Capacity	5 passengers or 818 litres or 907kg
Length	6.35m (20ft 10in)
Wingspan	11.98m (39ft 3in)
Height	2.79m (9ft 2in)
Weight empty	1,017kg (2,242lb)
Weight loaded	1,925kg (4,244lb)
Engine	1 x Textron Lycoming IO-540-K1A5 flat-6
Power	224kW (300hp)
Max speed	196kph (122mph)
Stall speed	73kph (45mph)
Range	1,297km (806 miles)
Ceiling	6,890m (22,600ft)

Transavia Airtruk.

IS IT A CAR? IS IT A PLANE?

Ever since the earliest days of aviation man has been obsessed by the idea of combining a car and an aircraft. Please note that I am not being sexist here by saying 'man' not 'people' because women are far too sensible to try anything so daft. (My wife insisted I include that comment here.) Some have been marginally successful – well, successful to the extent that they managed to fly – but none has achieved any commercial success. This is probably just as well, since the prospect of millions of car/planes flying freely over London, and dodging traffic from Heathrow, doesn't bear thinking about.

WATERMAN ARROWBILE

IT ACTUALLY PERFORMED WELL BUT DIDN'T ATTRACT MANY CUSTOMERS

The Waterman Arrowbile was a tailless two-seat, single-engine 'roadable' aircraft built in the United States in the late 1930s. It was one of the first attempts at a car/aircraft and performed reasonably well, but failed to attract sufficient customers. Only five were made, the last one as late as 1957.

Waido Waterman's first flying machine, unofficially known as the Waterman Whatsit, first flew in 1932. His second model was the Arrowplane, which looked much like the Arrowbile but was not intended to double up as a car, and was never planned for production. However, it was successful in the US government funded Vidal Safety Airplane competition, and this spurred Waterman to form the Waterman Arrowplane Company in 1935 with a view to producing a road-capable version of the Arrowplane. The result was the Arrowbile, officially the W-5, which was similar in appearance to the Arrowplane but had wings and a propeller that could be quickly detached for road use. For the Arrowbile the engine was changed from an air-cooled Menasco unit to a water-cooled 6-cylinder Studebaker one.

For road use the engine drove the rear wheels through a normal differential, and the vehicle was steered by its single front wheel. The steering wheel controlled direction both on the ground and in the air. The propeller could be left on for road use as it could be declutched from the engine and locked in position.

The Arrowbile was not a commercial success, and just five were produced, all slightly different.

Capacity	2
Length	5.89m (19ft 4in)
Wingspan	11.58m (38ft 0in)
Weight empty	880kg (1,941lb)
Weight loaded	1,134kg (2,500lb)
Engine	1 x Studebaker-Waterman 6-cyl in-line
Power	75kw (100hp)
Max speed	193kph (120mph)
Landing speed	72kph (45mph)
Max road speed	113kph (70mph)
Range (air)	563km (350 miles)

Waterman
Arrowbile.

AEROMOBIL

The AeroMobil, described by its makers AeroMobil s.r.o. as a 'roadable aircraft' rather than a 'flying car', is unique in two ways. Firstly, it represents the entire Slovakian aircraft industry. Secondly, whereas most attempts at flying cars, or 'roadable aircraft', look about as exciting as a second-hand Ford Mondeo, the AeroMobil appears as glamorous as a Bugatti Veyron.

Designed by Stefan Klein, the AeroMobil has taken twenty years to develop to the point of proof-of-concept, and first flew in 2013. The prototype, AeroMobil 1.0, was constructed in Bratislava by the AeroMobil Team led by co-founders Klein and Juraj Vaculik. The company is now on the fourth iteration, the 3.0, which was introduced at the Pioneers Festival 2014 in Vienna.

The latest version has folding wings, and is constructed of a steel frame covered in carbon fibre. It is still in development, and no final production date has been released.

Most prototype flying cars lack two ingredients needed for success. They don't look good and they fly even worse. Videos of the first flights of the AeroMobil 3.0 suggest there is still some way to go on the flying quality, but the company has certainly made a stunning-looking vehicle. If they get the flying spot on, they will almost certainly be onto a winner.

Capacity	2
Length	6.0m (19ft 8in)
Wingspan	8.32m (27ft 3in)
Engine	1 x Rotax 912 4-cyl horizontally opposed
Power	75kw (100hp)
Max airspeed	200kph (124mph)
Max road speed	160kph (99mph)
Stall speed	60kph (37mph)
Range (air)	700km (435 miles)
Range (road)	875km (545 miles)
Fuel used (air)	15 litres/hour (3.3 gallons/hour)
Fuel used (road)	8 litres per 100km (34.7 mpg)

AeroMobil. (Courtesy of Stefan Vadocz)

BEARDMORE INFLEXIBLE

WHAT IS THIS DOING IN THIS SECTION?

The Beardmore Inflexible is so obviously not a road-going aircraft, so what is it doing amongst the likes of the Skycar, the Aerocar and the Arrowbile?

There is a simple answer, albeit a rather stupid one. The only surviving piece of the single Inflexible built is one of its truly massive wheels. Faced with the massive wheel, which is preserved in the Science Museum, the onlooker might be left wondering whether it came from an aircraft or from some monumentally outsized truck.

The Inflexible was built in 1928 by William Beardmore & Company of Dalmuir in Scotland, and was a three-engined, all metal, stressed-skin prototype bomber. For its time the Inflexible was truly massive, having, for example, a wingspan 4.9m greater than that of the Boeing B-29 Superfortress bomber of the Second World War. However, with a take-off weight of 16,780kg (37,000lb) it was seriously underpowered, and desperately slow, and no interest was expressed by the government in production. The aircraft was dismantled in 1930, and the fuselage used to investigate the effect of corrosion on stressed light-alloy structures. And of course the massive wheel went to the Science Museum.

Length	23.02m (75ft 6in)
Wingspan	48.05m (157ft 6in)
Height	6.45m (21ft 2in)
Weight empty	11,022kg (24,301lb)
Weight loaded	16,783kg (37,000lb)
Engines	3 x Rolls Royce Condor II
Power	485kW (650hp) each
Max speed	175kph (109 mph)

Beardmore Inflexible.
(Courtesy of Flight Global)

115

CONVAIR 118

THE MOST 'CAR LIKE' OF THE CAR/AEROPLANES

The Convair 118 was different from most of the car/aircraft hybrids in that the car bit looked like a car and the aircraft bit looked like an aircraft. In fact it was really just a car and an aircraft joined together.

Convair's first flying car, the Model 116, first flew in 1946, and completed at least sixty-six test flights. The 118 appeared the following year, and included a new four-seat car where the 116 had been just a two-seater, and a more powerful flying engine, a 142kW (190hp) Lycoming unit. The car engine was still a modest 19kW (25hp) Crosley.

The plan was to mass-produce the 118, with sales figures of 160,000 being talked about, and a price tag of $1,500. However, everything did not run smoothly. Three days after

Wingspan	10.49m (34ft 5in)
Height	2.54m (8ft 4in)
Weight empty	691kg (1,524lb)
Weight loaded	1,157kg (2,550lb)
Engines	1 x Lycoming O-435C air-cooled flat-6
	1 x Crosley air-cooled
Power	140kW (190hp) air
	19kW (25hp) road
Cruising speed	201kph (125mph) in the air

the first test flight, the test pilot had to make a forced landing when he ran out of fuel, the landing wrecking the car. It turned out he had read the car's fuel gauge by mistake, and that the aircraft fuel tank was almost empty. A 'second' prototype was built using a new car body with the same wing, and this flew for the first time in January 1948. However, enthusiasm for the project within Convair waned and development was stopped.

TERRAFUGIA TRANSITION

'HELPING HUMANITY ACHIEVE A NEW DIMENSION OF PERSONAL FREEDOM'

The subtitle above is how the company positions the Transition. However, I do fear slightly for the safety of humanity if too large a proportion of it actually achieves the desired 'new dimension of personal freedom', particularly if they achieve this over my house.

The Transition is the first product from Terrafugia, a company set up in 2006 by a group of engineers from MIT. The team won the MIT Business Plan Competition in 2006, which provided the initial capital for the business. Incidentally, the name Terrafugia was derived from the Latin for 'escape the earth'.

The Transition looks much more like a car than most of its rivals, and also it is fully self-contained, with the wings folding alongside the body for road use.

The Transition's first flight was in March 2009 at Plattsburgh International Airport in upstate New York. By April 2014 twelve two-person flights had been completed. The first customer delivery was originally planned for 2012, but delays for further development have pushed this back, and deliveries are now planned to begin in 2016.

The Transition converts from a fully street-legal car to an aircraft in less than one minute, and is in fact the only aircraft to meet full Federal Motor Vehicle Safety Standards.

The cost is currently predicted to be around $279,000, and reservations are being accepted now. Terrafugia is already developing a second model, the TF-X, which will be a vertical take-off aircraft and a plug-in hybrid car.

Length	5.72m (18ft 9in)
Wingspan	8.08m (26ft 6in)
Height	2.03m (6ft 8in)
Max load	227kg (500lb)
Engine	Rotax 912iS
Power	75kW (100hp)
Cruising speed	160kph (100mph)
Max road speed	110kph (70mph)
Range	660km (410 miles)
Take-off roll	518m (1700ft) to clear 15m (50ft) obstacle
Fuel used (flying)	5 gallons per hour
Fuel used (road)	6.7 litres per 100km (35mpg)
Fuel capacity	87 litres (23 gallons)

Terrafugia Transition.

TAYLOR AEROCAR

DON'T LEAVE YOUR WINGS BEHIND, TAKE THEM WITH YOU

Aerocar International's Aerocar, often referred to as the Taylor Aerocar, was designed by Moulton Taylor and first appeared in 1949. The Aerocar adopted a slightly different solution from the other car/aircraft hybrids in that when on the road all the 'flying bits' are towed behind on a trailer. The design allowed the conversion from car to aircraft to be completed in around five minutes by one person. The drive for the pusher propeller was concealed behind the rear number plate.

The same engine drove the car and the plane, this being a Lycoming unit. On the road drive was to the front wheels, and once airborne the road transmission was simply left in neutral.

The Aerocar gained civil air certification in 1956, and Taylor then entered into a deal with Ling-Temco-Vought for serial production on the condition that he was able to attract 500 orders. Unfortunately he was only able to find customers for around half that amount, so production never started.

In many ways the Taylor Aerocar was the most successful and practical of the car/aircraft hybrids.

Taylor Aerocar.

Crew	1
Capacity	1 passenger
Length	6.55m (21ft 6in)
Wingspan	10.36m (34ft 0in)
Height	2.29m (7ft 6in)
Weight empty	680kg (1,500lb)
Weight loaded	953kg (2,100lb)
Engine	1 x Lycoming O-320 air-cooled flat-4
Power	107kW (143hp)
Cruising speed	156kph (97mph)
Max speed	188kph (117mph) in the air
Stall speed	80kph (50mph)
Range	483km (300 miles)
Service ceiling	3,658m (12,000ft)

PARAJET SKYCAR

A FLYING CAR IN A CLASS OF ITS OWN

The Parajet Skycar is quite unique. It is a flying car that utilises a ParaWing, or parafoil, attached to a road-legal car to achieve sustained level flight. The great advantage of the ParaWing concept is that in the case of engine failure the Skycar will glide slowly and safely to the ground. In addition, in the case of

Crew	2 driver/pilot
Capacity	1 passenger
Weight empty	420kg (925lb)
Engine	1 x 1,000cc EcoBoost Direct Injection Turbo
Power	92kW (125bhp)
Max road speed	185kph (115mph)
0–100kph	4.3 seconds
Max air speed	88.5kph (55mph)
Take-off speed	59.5kph (37mph)
Cruising speed	56.3kph (35mph)
Range	321.8km (200 miles)
Ceiling	4,500m (15,000ft)
Restricted ceiling	3,000m (10,000ft)
Unit cost	£60,000 ($98,000)

Parajet Skycar. (Courtesy of Parajet & Nick Wilson)

catastrophic failure of the 'wing', of the connection to the car, or a mid-air collision, an emergency reserve parachute can be deployed to bring the car safely to earth. It takes just three minutes to convert from a car to an aircraft, and can take off in under 200m.

Parajet position the Skycar as the 'ultimate recreational sports vehicle', part all-terrain buggy part light aircraft.

One major difference between the Skycar and other flying cars is that the Skycar has, on the ground, supercar performance from its 1,000cc EcoBoost Direct Injection Turbo engine with DOHC and four valves per cylinder. The 0–62mph (0–100kph) time is just 4.2 seconds, and the top road speed is 185kph (115mph). Unlike all the other flying cars, the Skycar is much faster on the ground than in the air. The suspension is independent all round, and the gearbox is a pneumatic paddle-shift four-speed unit. It is equipped with two FIA Approved Race Seats.

Parajet Skycar. (Courtesy of Parajet & Nick Wilson)

120

MOLLER SKYCARS

ONE MAN'S LIFELONG OBSESSION

Moller Skycar.

Paul Moller was a man on a mission. For more than fifty years he has been trying to develop an inexpensive 'flying car', his vision being that they would be used just like cars. However, given that there are 2.5 million cars in London, for example, the idea of 2.5 million independently flown skycars whizzing over the city doesn't bear thinking about!

Moller's original idea for the Skycar, the M200, was a perfectly round vehicle powered by no fewer than eight Wankel engines, with the passengers sitting under a clear bubble in the middle. Most of the flying would be computer controlled, with the 'pilot' just telling the machine where to go. Moller began advertising for financial backers in the mid 1960s, with a 'promise' that the Skycar would cost under $100,000 and would be ready within a few years. Moller claimed the M200 had completed over 200 test flights, but no evidence of this was ever forthcoming. Indeed there was no evidence the M200 itself ever existed.

Around $200 million and forty years later the Skycar is no nearer becoming a reality. The latest version, the M400 shown in the photograph, relies on just four Wankel engines and is a four-seater. Moller claims the M400 can hover at an altitude of 15ft whilst tethered, a little low for a 'sky' car. Development work appears to have ceased. Moller's repeated unrealistic and unsubstantiated claims for the Skycar resulted in Moller being sued for fraud by the Securities & Exchange Commission in 2003.

In 2006 Moller attempted to sell the only prototype M200 on eBay, with a reserve of $3.5 million, but it failed to sell. The whole Moller venture with his Skycars has been dubbed 'physical product vapourware', which I suppose is a nice technical way to say 'a load of hot air'.

Crew	1
Passengers	3
Length	5.9m (19ft 4in)
Wingspan	2.6m (8ft 6in)
Wing area	254m²
Height	2.3m (7ft 7in)
Weight empty	1,088kg (2,394lb)
Engines	4 x Rotapower 500 Wankel
Power	134kW (180hp) each
Max speed	530kph (claimed) 0kph (actual)
Service ceiling	10,973m (claimed) 5m (actual)

SOMETIMES DESIGNERS JUST FORGET THINGS

Looking at some of the aircraft designs covered in this book it is difficult not to believe that there are some serious memory problems in some aeronautical design offices. Maybe it's early-onset Alzheimer's, or maybe the designers simply became distracted by an alien spacecraft touching down in the car park outside looking for a good pizza takeaway. Whatever the cause, there are so many examples of aircraft plans leaving the design office devoid of just a few fairly trivial items such as wings, tailplanes, cockpits, landing gear and so on, those little luxury extras which make the pilot's life just that little bit more comfortable.

In the case of the Northrop HL-10 the designers appear to have forgotten virtually everything apart from the fuselage. But there is a good reason for this. The HL-10 was one of five heavyweight 'lifting bodies' used by NASA to study and validate the idea of manoeuvring and landing a low-lift-over-drag vehicle for re-entry from space. The 'HL' denotes horizontal landing and the '10' simply means it was the tenth design considered by NASA.

It had no wings as such, the whole body forming an inverted aerofoil, the only concession to 'normality' for a plane being the tail and vestigial angled tailplanes.

Unlike the Space Shuttle that was eventually used for re-entry, the HL-10 did have a power plant in the form of an 8,000lbf rocket.

Finally, the HL-10 does have one very strange claim to fame. In an episode of *The Six Million Dollar Man*, entitled 'The Deadly Replay', the HL-10 is identified as the craft in which Colonel Steve Austin was travelling when he crashed, necessitating the rebuilding of his body as the bionic man. The HL-10 also featured in the opening credits of the show.

Northrop HL-10.

Cockpit Crew	1 (doesn't have to be bionic)
Length	6.45m (21ft 2in)
Wingspan	4.15m (13ft 7in)
Height	2.92m (9ft 7in)
Weight empty	2,397kg (5,273lb)
Weight loaded	2,721kg (5,986lb)
Engine	1 x Reaction Motors XLR-11 4-chamber rocket
Thrust	35.7kN (8,000lbf)
Max speed	1,976kph (Mach 0.92)
Range	72km
Ceiling	27,524m
Fuel capacity	1,604kg

LEDUC RAMJET

THE PILOT SITS INSIDE THE ENGINE!

The Leduc Ramjet was the brainchild of Frenchman René Leduc, and was one of the first planes ever to fly using only a ramjet. It was essentially a research aircraft to explore the use of such engines.

The Leduc was unusual in a number of ways. Firstly almost the entire craft is the engine itself, and basically consists of two concentric tubes. The space between the tubes provides the inlet for the engine.

Secondly, being a ramjet, it cannot take off under its own power, as a ramjet must be moving through the air before it will work. So the Leduc was carried aloft by a Sud-Est Languedoc mothership before being released at altitude.

Thirdly, and most bizarrely, the pilot actually sat inside the centre of the engine, in a tiny cockpit contained within the inner tube. With virtually no chance of ejecting from this position, and what must have been an unbelievably uncomfortable hot and noisy environment, it must have helped if the pilot was quite incredibly brave, or maybe just slightly intellectually challenged.

Leduc Ramjet.

Cockpit Crew	1 (bravery or just stupidity helps)
Length	10.25m (33ft 8in)
Wingspan	10.52m (34ft 6in)
Weight empty	1,700kg (3,740lb)
Weight loaded	2,800kg (6,160lb)
Engine	1 x Leduc ramjet
Thrust	15.7kN (3,520lbf)
Max speed	800kph

MARTIN MARIETTA X-24A & X-24B

FORGETTING THINGS CAN BECOME A HABIT

The Martin Marietta X-24A and X-24B serve to demonstrate that forgetting little details, such as wings, cannot be dismissed simply as an accidental oversight. It seems some aircraft manufacturers make a career of it.

The X-24A made its appearance in 1969, just three years after the very similar Northrop HL-10. Like the Northrop it was an experimental 'lifting body' designed to test the concept of unpowered re-entry and landing later used on the Space Shuttle. Lifting bodies are designed to fly without wings, gaining all the lift from the shape of the body itself. The X-24A was a fat, short teardrop shape with vertical fins for control. The first, unpowered, gliding flight was made in April 1969, and then in March 1970 it made its first powered flight being drop-launched at 13,700m (45,000ft) from a B-52 bomber. During a series of twenty-eight test

Martin X-24A.

Martin X-24B.

	X-24A	X-24B
Cockpit Crew	1	1
Length	7.47m (24ft 6in)	11.43m (37ft 6in)
Wingless-span	3.51m (11ft 6in)	5.79m (19ft 0in)
Height	2.92m (9ft 7in)	2.92m (9ft 7in)
Weight empty	2,885kg (6,360lb)	3,855kg (8,500lb)
Weight loaded	4,853kg (10,700lb)	5,350kg (11,800lb)
Engines	1 x Reaction Motors	1 x Reaction Motors
	XLR-11 rocket	XLR-11 rocket
Thrust	37.7kN (8,480lbf)	37.7kN (8,480lbf)
Max speed	1,667kph (1,036mph)	1,873kph (1,164mph)
Range	72km (45miles)	72km (45miles)
Ceiling	21,763m (71,407ft)	22,590m (74,130ft)
Number built	1	1

flights the X-24A used its rocket engine to climb up to 21,600m (71,400ft) before gliding back to Earth. On these test flights speeds of 1,667kph (1,036mph) were reached.

The X-24B was not actually a new aircraft; instead it was the X-24A recycled. The fat and bulbous X-24A was slimmed down and rebuilt resembling a paper dart. The same rocket engine was retained, but the X-24B grew in size, and in particular was 53 per cent longer. The new shape gave a higher top speed than before, reaching 1,873kph (1,164mph), some 200kph faster than in its first incarnation. The X-24B flew a total of thirty-six times, and is now preserved at the US Air Force National Museum in Ohio.

Between 1972 and 1978 several proposals were put forward for an X-24C, but these came to nothing. The most adventurous idea around this time in relation to space re-entry was the L-301 from the Lockheed Skunk Works, which was to use scramjets to reach Mach 8.

SNECMA FLYING COLÉOPTÈRE C450

THE DESIGNER FORGOT NEARLY EVERYTHING

In the case of the Coléoptère C450 it looks as though the designer forgot nearly everything, as it has no wing, no tail fin, no tailplane, and no undercarriage … unless you count four tiny castors as 'undercarriage'.

After the war, when the German air force was permitted to be re-established around 1958, there was concern in Britain and France that Germany was not ordering their aircraft, but instead looked to the US and bought the F-104 Starfighter (itself covered in this book under 'Planes Perfectly Designed to Kill the People Flying Them'). The Coléoptère was developed as an aircraft that might appeal to Germany given that its vertical take-off and landing meant it didn't require proper air strips.

One very unusual feature of the aircraft was the tilting seat for the pilot. Given that the cockpit windows did not tilt, it must have made take-off and landing quite a daunting experience … or would have done if the Coléoptère had survived long enough to actually make take-offs and landings.

One prototype was produced and tested. However, the Coléoptère proved to be extremely unstable and very dangerous to fly. The prototype crashed on its first free, untethered, flight and was destroyed, though the pilot survived. The project was not continued. The photograph shows the Coléoptère being unloaded from a lorry, which bears more than a passing resemblance to a skip truck. This only serves to emphasise the fact that the Coléoptère was complete rubbish.

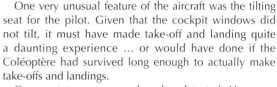

Cockpit Crew	1
Length	8.02m (26ft 3in)
Diameter	3.20m (10ft 6in)
Weight loaded	3,000kg (6,600lb) approx
Engine	1 x SNECMA Atar 101E.V
Thrust	3,700kg
Max speed	800kph (estimate)
Range	unknown
Ceiling	3,000m (theoretical), 75m (actual)
Danger	known and very high
Number built	one too many

SNECMA Coléoptère.

DESIGNERS WERE FORGETTING THINGS AS EARLY AS 1948

Several years before the guys at Martin Marietta started forgetting things like wings, the designers at McDonnell had already gone one better and designed the Goblin, where it seems they almost completely forgot to build a fuselage, and left out another rather desirable feature for an aircraft, namely an undercarriage.

However, there was good reason for their frugality in providing the luxury extras like wings and landing gear. The Goblin was intended to be dropped from the bomb bay of the Convair B-36 bomber, itself featured in this book. It was a so-called 'parasite fighter'. The advantage of the parasite approach was that it avoided the problems of the limited range of the existing interceptors. The idea was that the fighter would be dropped from the bomber, intercept the enemy, and then return to the bomber using a large hook to engage with a 'trapeze' underneath.

The programme was not a success for the following reasons:

- Pilots didn't like the idea of being treated like a bomb.
- The retrieval process was extremely hazardous, mainly caused by serious turbulence from the retrieval hook. It may or may not be true that the Goblin test pilots always wore brown trousers.
- The Goblin did not have any landing gear, so a ground landing was never a back-up option.
- It was much slower than the enemy fighters it was designed to intercept.
- During initial testing in a wind tunnel the testers accidently dropped the first prototype from a height of 40ft, writing it off, which did nothing to speed up development.

The programme stopped after just two prototypes had been built.

Cockpit Crew	1
Length	4.5m (14ft 10in)
Wingspan	6.4m (21ft 1in)
Height	2.5m (8ft 3in)
Weight empty	1,700kg (3,740lb)
Weight loaded	2,050kg (4,550lb)
Engine	1 x Westinghouse XJ34-WE-22 turbojet
Power	13.3 kN (3,000lbf)
Max speed	1,069km (650mph)
Ceiling	14,600m (48,000ft)

McDonnell XF-85 Goblin.

CONVAIR XFY POGO

IF NORTHROP, MARTIN AND MCDONNELL CAN DO IT, SO CAN CONVAIR!

In the early–mid 1950s it seems to have been all the rage amongst aircraft manufacturers to have some way-out design with, for example, no wings, no tail, no under-carriage, or even to place the pilot inside the engine itself or drop the plane with the pilot inside like a bomb. Convair did not want to be left out, and so introduced their own way-out design, but for the icing on the cake they also gave it a stupid name: Pogo.

The XFY Pogo was a vertical-take-off-and-landing (VTOL) craft with four delta wings symmetrically arranged around its fuselage, and a pair of contra-rotating propellers. It was intended as a high-performance fighter capable of operating from quite small warships. It proved very difficult to fly, especially when landing, when the pilot had to look backwards over his shoulder whilst operating the throttle.

The XFY was like no other plane before. Nothing of similar size, weight or power had ever tried to take off and land vertically. So nervous were the guys at Convair that for the first test flights in 1954 the craft was tethered by no fewer than five security cables in case the pilot lost control.

Later test flights revealed serious flaws in the design. One flaw was the lack of spoilers or air brakes, which meant it was very difficult to slow the Pogo down prior to landing. This, coupled with the extremely tricky landing procedure, meant that the Pogo could only ever be operated by the very top flight pilots. It was also simply not fast enough, and the surplus thrust over take-off weight was only 750lbf, making vertical take-offs highly challenging. The Pogo's last flight was in 1956.

Crew	1
Length	10.66m (34ft 11.7in)
Wingspan	8.43m (27ft 7in)
Weight empty	5,310kg (11,700lb)
Weight loaded	7,370kg (16,250lb)
Engine	1 x Allison YT40-A-16 turboprop
Power	4,100kW (5,500hp, 17,000lbf thrust)
Max speed	980kph (610mph)
Range	640km (400 miles)
Ceiling	13,300m (43,600ft)
Armament	4 x 20mm cannon or
	48 x 70mm Mk 4 Folding Fin Aerial Rockets

Convair XFY Pogo.

DOUGLAS X-3 STILETTO

ALL STYLE, NO SUBSTANCE

The Douglas X-3 Stiletto certainly looked the part, with its slender fuselage, very long pointed nose and tiny razor-thin wings. It looked as though it would smash through Mach 3 and climb to the edge of space before breakfast, without even working up a sweat.

But there was a problem … a big problem. Whilst designed to exceed Mach 2, it was so grossly under-powered that it couldn't even reach Mach 1 in level flight, the sound barrier requiring a steep 30° dive. In spite of its futuristic and aggressive looks, it was in reality little faster than the Convair Pogo.

It had been intended as a vehicle for testing advanced Mach 2 capable turbojets, and the planned engine was the Westinghouse J46. But these were unable to meet the thrust, size and weight criteria set and so less powerful Westinghouse J34s were fitted producing only 21.8kN (4,900lbf) of thrust compared to the 31.3kN (7,000lbf) required.

It wasn't a total disaster, however, but for a totally unforeseen reason. The aircraft was switched to research on lateral and directional stability. On a test flight in 1954 the pilot made an abrupt left roll at Mach 0.92 as intended, but the aircraft also pitched and yawed violently, and was nearly lost. The pilot managed to regain control and land safely. The phenomenon of 'roll inertia coupling' had been discovered, whereby a manoeuvre in one axis will cause unintentional manoeuvres in one or two other planes. A research pro-gramme was started by NASA to understand the problem and find a solution. To this extent the underpowered Stiletto had a useful career.

Crew	1
Length	20.3m (66ft 9in)
Wingspan	6.9m (22ft 8in)
Weight empty	7,310kg (16,120lb)
Weight loaded	10,810kg (23,840lb)
Engines	2 x Westinghouse J34 afterburning turbojet
Power	21.6kN (4,850lbf) each with afterburners
Max speed	1,125kph (700mph)
Range	800km (497 miles)
Ceiling	11,600m (38,000ft)

Douglas X-3 Stiletto.

BOEING X-48B

THE FLYING WING ... FORTUNATELY AIRLINE PASSENGERS WERE SPARED THIS FATE

Boeing had in the past studied the 'blended wing' design for possible passenger aircraft. This would have placed passengers inside an enormous windowless 'amphitheatre' within the flying wing. Not surprisingly passenger reaction when shown a mock-up was not very positive to say the least.

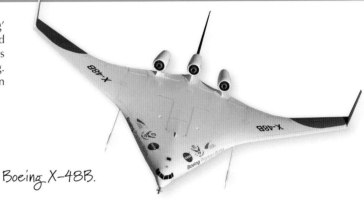

Boeing X-48B.

Crew	0
Wingspan	6.22m (20ft 5in)
Weight loaded	227kg (500lb)
Engines	3 x JetCat P200 turbojet
Power	0.23kN (52lbf) each
Max speed	219kph (136mph)
Range	40 minutes
Ceiling	3,048m (10,000ft)

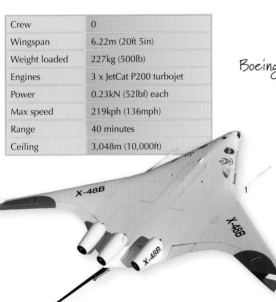

However, Boeing continued research on the concept for military aircraft, since the blended wing had many advantages, including greater range, better fuel economy, reliability, manufacturing costs and lifecycle benefits.

The X-48B was one of a series of unmanned, scaled-down aircraft to research the 'tail-less flying wing' concept. It was powered by three tiny turbojets mounted on top of the 'wing', and weighed in at just 227kg (500lb).

Overall the little X-48B was very successful as a research vehicle. It is, however, fortunate for the public that the concept was not rolled out to passenger jets, otherwise the 600–800 passengers on the Airbus A380 might today be sitting in a cabin rather like the interior of the Barbican Hall.

131

DORNIER DO-34 KIEBITZ

AN AIRCRAFT WHERE THEY FORGOT ALMOST EVERYTHING!

It is a little unfair to say the designers forgot nearly everything when designing the Kiebitz (which incidentally means 'lapwing' in German). It was designed as an unmanned surveillance platform, and so merely needed to travel vertically up and vertically down. It didn't even have a fuel tank, as fuel was intended to be pumped up to it via an 'umbilical cord'.

It was based on the small single-seat helicopter, the Do-32U, with tip-jet propulsion driving the rotor. With just an engine and a rotor it was little more than a flying dustbin, which it actually looked quite like. Having no tail or tail rotor, to prevent the dustbin rotating madly instead of the rotor, it was equipped with twin exhaust nozzles, clearly seen in the photograph.

All the systems remained on the launch platform, which was a conventional army truck. The first Lapwing was limited to 200m height, but the army required 300m where it would be able to 'see' for around 65km. Dornier had the idea of building a version capable of attaining 1,000m, which would have been unfettered, as it was not practical to pump fuel to such a height. In the end the military decided that reconnaissance would be better done from conventional aircraft, and the programme ceased.

Crew	0
Length	It's round!
Rotor diameter	8.4m (27ft 7in)
Weight empty	350kg (770lb)
Weight loaded	550kg (1,210lb)
Engine	1 x Allison 250-C20 turbine
Power	309kw (414hp)
Endurance	24 hours
Ascent rate	300m in 6 minutes
Ceiling	300m (1,000ft)
Armament	none
Number built	2

Dornier Do-34 Kiebitz.

KAMOV KA-26

DID THE DESIGNER LOSE INTEREST HALF WAY THROUGH?

Looking at the photograph of the Ka-26 it is easy to conclude that the designer somehow lost interest in it once he'd done the cockpit, engines and rotors. But in reality it is a remarkably successful and flexible design.

The reason the Ka-26 looks unfinished in the photograph is that it is, in one way at least, unfinished. It was designed to accept different

Kamov
Ka-26.

Crew	2
Capacity	6 passengers
Length	7.75m (25ft 5in)
Rotor diameter	2 x 13.00m (42ft 8in)
Weight empty	1,950kg (4,300lb)
Weight loaded	3,250kg (7,170lb)
Engines	2 x Vedeneyev M-144 radial piston
Power	239kW (325hp) each
Endurance	3 hours 42 minutes
Max speed	170kph (105mph)
Range	400km (248 miles)
Ceiling	3,000m (9,840ft)
Number built	816

removable boxes behind the cockpit, mainly ones for passengers, medevac equipment or for crop dusting. I do, however, wonder how secure the six passengers must have felt knowing they were travelling in a removable box, which, I presume, could be released in mid-air if the pilot pulled the wrong lever.

The Ka-26 is also unusual in two ways. Firstly, unlike most modern helicopters, it uses two radial piston engines which, whilst more responsive than turboshafts, require much more maintenance; also on the Ka-26 they are required to operate at around 95 per cent maximum power, leaving little in reserve for emergencies. The high loading leads to frequent failures of the drive shafts.

Secondly, it uses a pair of contra-rotating rotors. Interestingly this results in a delicate airflow pattern under the rotors, which has proved ideal for crop dusting.

Oh, incidentally, the NATO code word for the Ka-26 is 'Hoodlum'. I've never fully understood why NATO adopts unusual code names for aircraft from the old Soviet Bloc countries.

VERTICAL TAKE-OFF ODDITIES

The desire to take off vertically, usually to save space by doing without runways and other bulky things, has resulted in its fair share of oddities. We are all very familiar with one solution, the helicopter, which itself has produced some first-rate oddities such as the helicopter which folds up for storage in a torpedo tube. But the other solution, that of morphing from vertical flight to normal horizontal flight, has produced some wonderfully obscure and strange beasts.

SIKORSKY S-72 'X-WING'

A SCHIZOPHRENIC AIRCRAFT ... IT CAN'T DECIDE IF IT'S A HELICOPTER OR A FIXED-WING AIRCRAFT

The S-72 'X-Wing' was an experimental hybrid helicopter/fixed-wing aircraft developed by Sikorsky for NASA and the US Army. Was it possible that two designers worked on it, one on the day shift thinking he was designing a helicopter, and the other on the night shift believing it was to have fixed wings? When the drawing-office manager realised what was going on he was too embarrassed to admit the mistake and disappoint one of the team, and so he allowed the strange hybrid to come into being.

But perhaps an even more extraordinary feature on the X-Wing was its novel 'crew emergency extraction system'. When activated, this system fired explosive bolts that severed the main rotor blades, blew off 'egress panels' from the cockpit roof, and then ejected the crew by the use of rockets. It makes you wonder whether the crew might not have preferred to take their chances in a crash instead.

It was intended to take off vertically like a helicopter, and transition to forward flight at which point the rotor could be stopped and act like wings. Unlike a normal helicopter, the rotor blades were fixed rather than tilting as they rotated. In theory this should result in the whole thing flipping over as the blade moving forward gave more lift than the one going backwards. To get round this slight technical issue compressed air was blown out of the edge of the blades, using computerised valves, to maintain balance. In the end, the whole thing was deemed too complicated and the development programme was axed.

Crew	2–3
Length	21.5m (70ft 6in)
Wingspan	18.9m (62ft 0in)
Height	4.42m (14ft 6in)
Weight empty	9,480kg (20,856lb)
Weight loaded	11,815kg (25,993lb)
Engines	2 x General Electric TF34-GE-400A turbofans
	2 x General Electric T58-GE-5 turbojets
Cruising speed	258kph
Max speed	370kph with auxiliary jets
	296kph without auxiliary jets
Number built	2

Sikorsky X-Wing.

DORNIER DO-31

AN INTRIGUING BY-PRODUCT OF THE COLD WAR

In the early 1960s the Luftwaffe had become increasingly concerned that their airfields were vulnerable to attack from the Eastern Bloc forces. They started looking at different ways to deploy aircraft, including using the Autobahns for STOVL (short take-off vertical landing) planes.

Early trials included modifying F-104 Starfighters to be rocket launched from ramps and recovered using aircraft-carrier-type arresting gear. The Starfighter was scary enough under normal operations, so how an F-104 with a rocket 'up its bum' would have been received by the pilots is anybody's guess.

Marginally more sensible was the Do-31, an experimental West German vertical take-off and landing (VTOL) aircraft built by Dornier. It was designed in response to a NATO specification. Vertical lift was provided by no fewer than eight turbojets mounted in wing tip pods, whilst forward motion came from two turbofans.

The Do-31 was the first, and so far the only, vertical take-off jet transport plane ever built. The project was cancelled in 1970, largely because the large drag and weight of the engine pods reduced payload and range compared to more conventional formats.

Crew	2
Passengers	36 troops or 24 casualty stretchers
Length	20.53m (67ft 4in)
Wingspan	18m (59ft 1in)
Height	8.53m (28ft 0in)
Weight loaded	22,453kg (49,397lb)
Max take-off weight	27,422kg (60,328lb)
Engines	2 x Rolls-Royce Pegasus BE 53/2 turbofans
	8 x Rolls-Royce RB162-4D vertical turbojet lift engines
Power	294.46kN (66,197lbf)
Max speed	730kph
Range	1,800km
Service ceiling	10,700m
Number built	3

Dornier Do-31.

HUGHES XH-17 'FLYING CRANE'

A HELICOPTER COBBLED TOGETHER FROM THE PARTS BIN ... AND NOT VERY WELL

The XH-17 'Flying Crane' was the first helicopter produced by Hughes Aircraft. The enormous twin-blade main rotor enabled the XH-17 to lift 23,000kg. In order to speed up construction Hughes Aircraft seems to have gone on a raid of the parts bins. The front wheels came from a B-25 Mitchell, the rear wheels from a C-54 Skymaster, the fuel tank was a bomb-bay mounted unit from a B-29 Superfortress, the cockpit came from a Waco CG-15, and the tail rotor was scavenged from a Sikorsky H-19. It is no surprise, therefore, that it looks like the 'ugly duckling' of the helicopter world.

The XH-17 first flew in October 1952, and was retired just three years later. It proved too cumbersome, too inefficient and had too short a range of just 64km to warrant any further development. Just one was built. However, the 'Flying Crane' still holds the record for the world's largest rotor system. It may also hold the undisputed crown for the ugliest helicopter of all time.

An unusual feature of the XH-17 was the propulsion system. The two GE turbojets blew hot air through ducts in the rotor to the rotor tips, where fuel was injected and produced thrust ... a form of wing-tip afterburner. With this system, where the rotor is driven from its tips, there is little torque reaction and as a result the helicopter could manage with a very small tail rotor. However, this method of propulsion proved very inefficient and heavy on fuel, giving the very disappointing range already mentioned. The XH-17 was withdrawn and scrapped in 1955.

Crew	3
Length	16.25m (53ft 4in)
Rotor diameter	39.62m (130ft 0in)
Height	9.17m (30ft 1in)
Weight empty	12,956kg (28,503lb)
Weight loaded	14,184kg (31,205lb)
Useful load	4,665kg (10,263lb)
Max take-off weight	19,731kg (43,408lb)
Engines	2 x General Electric J35 turbojets
Cruising speed	137kph
Max speed	145kph
Range	64km
Service ceiling	3,995m

Hughes XH-17.

FLYING BEDSTEAD

NOT SO GOOD FOR A NIGHT'S SLEEP, THOUGH

The Rolls-Royce Thrust-Measuring Rig (TMR), to give the 'Flying Bedstead' its proper name, was a Vertical Take Off and Landing (VTOL) vehicle developed by Rolls-Royce in the 1950s to conduct research into VTOL technology. It was about as basic as a flying machine can be: two powerful jet engines strapped together back-to-back horizontally and … well, virtually nothing else except a can of petrol and a couple of nozzles.

Two TMRs were built, first taking to the air in 1953, although remaining tethered to the ground. The first free flight was the following year, with R.T. Shepherd, Rolls-Royce's chief test pilot, at the controls. The TMR's thrust was only just greater than its weight, and this made flying very tricky. This, combined with slow throttle

Crew	1 (pilot preferably not asleep)
Length	8.53m (28ft 0in)
Wingspan	4.26m (14ft 0in)
Height	3.86m (12ft 8in)
Weight empty	2,720kg (5,984lb)
Weight loaded	3,400kg (7,480lb)
Engines	2 x Rolls-Royce Nene turbojets
Power	18kN (4,047lbf) each
Cruising speed	0kph
Max speed	0kph
Range	0km
Service ceiling	just a few metres
Number built	2

Flying Bedstead.

control, no inherent stability, and a complex system of nozzles to direct exhaust to steer the thing, made it only marginally easier to control in flight than a double bed.

The Flying Bedstead was used to test turbojet engines for lifting purposes and to develop control systems for aircraft using VTOL technology. This led to the first true British VTOL aircraft, the Short SC1, which in turn led to the Harrier jump jet we know today.

CURTISS-WRIGHT VZ-7

WAS THIS THE UNIDENTIFIED FLYING TOAST RACK?

The VZ-7 was a VTOL quad-rotor helicopter designed by Curtiss-Wright for the US Army, and was intended to be seen as a flying jeep. Two prototypes were made for the US Army in 1956. The VZ-7 had a fuselage that contained the pilot's seat, the fuel tanks and all the flight controls. There were four horizontal rotors, two on each side of the fuselage, and below the level of the victim, sorry pilot. Originally these rotors had been enclosed by shrouds, but in the pre-production prototype these were removed creating what must be, by any standards, the scariest and most dangerous aerial shredding machine of all time. It was to be hoped that the pilot, upon alighting, only walked forwards from the craft, otherwise there was a serious risk that he'd be minced to pieces.

The VZ-7 was controlled by changing the speed and hence the thrust from the four rotors. By all accounts it was fairly easy to fly. Although it performed well during tests, it failed to achieve the US Army's rigorous standards, and it was returned to the manufacturer when trials were completed.

The craft still exists at the US Army Aviation Museum but is not on public display.

Curtiss-Wright VZ-7.

Crew	1
Length	5.18m (17ft 0in)
Wingspan	not relevant
Width	4.87m (16ft 0in)
Height	2.83m (9ft 3in)
Engine	1 x Turbomeca Artouste IIB turboshaft
Power	320kW (429hp)
Max speed	51kph
Service ceiling	60m
Number built	2

MIL V-12

QUITE SIMPLY THE LARGEST HELICOPTER EVER BUILT

The Mil V-12 remains to this day the largest helicopter ever built, continuing a Soviet desire to have the 'biggest in the air' in all aviation categories.

Design studies for the giant helicopter started back in 1959, and in 1961 Mil was instructed to design and develop a helicopter capable of lifting 20–25 metric tonnes. It was required to have a similar cargo hold capacity to the fixed-wing Antonov An-22, and be capable of carrying the largest intercontinental ballistic missiles of the time.

The major limitation was rotor format. A single rotor was ruled out as not feasible, and tandem twin rotors similar to the US Chinook revealed undisclosed technical problems, so the transverse rotor layout was adopted. The twin rotors were mounted, together with their engines, at the end of 30m-span 'wings', the first by Mil but not the first helicopter to adopt this format, Kamov and Focke-Wulf having used

it for their Ka-22 Vintokryl and Fw 61 respectively.

At the front of the aircraft a two-storey cockpit housed the pilot, co-pilot flight engineer and electrical engineer on the 'ground floor', and

the navigator and radio operator on the 'first floor'. At the rear access to the vast cargo area was by means of huge clamshell doors and a retractable ramp. There were also five separate cargo doors on the sides.

Crew	6
Capacity	196 passengers
Length	37m (121ft 4in)
Wingspan	67m (across rotors) (219ft 10in)
Height	12.5m (41ft 0in)
Weight empty	69,100kg (152,020lb)
Max weight	97,000kg (213,400lb)
Freight compartment	28.15m x 4.4m x 4.4m
Engines	4 x Soloviev D-25VF turboshaft engines
Power	4,800kW (6,436hp) each
Cruising speed	240kph
Max speed	260kph
Range	500km
Service ceiling	3,500m
Number built	2

Mil V–12.

One interesting feature of the V-12 is that the two rotors overlapped by about 3m. In order to ensure the rotors didn't collide they were linked by a shaft across the width of the 'wing', and in the event of engine failure on one side the remaining engines could rotate both rotors at reduced speed … well, that was the theory anyway, and luckily it's never had to be proven.

The prototypes performed very well, and still hold many world records for helicopters, including not only the largest ever built but also many records for the heaviest payload ever lifted, including, for example, lifting 31,030kg to a height of 2,951m. However, in spite of its obvious technical prowess and success, the Soviet Air Force refused to accept the V-12 for state acceptance trials for many reasons, the main one being that the very need for its existence, the rapid movement of strategic ballistic missiles, no longer existed. But both prototypes still exist, one at the Mil helicopter factory near Moscow, and the other at the Monino Air Force Museum 50km east of Moscow, where it is on public display.

MIL MI-10

INSPIRED BY A DADDY-LONG-LEGS?

Looking at the Mil Mi-10 it is hard not to conclude that the chief designer at Mil Moscow Helicopter Plant was bored one day, wondering what wonderful new helicopter to design when suddenly a daddy-long-legs flew in through the window and settled on his drawing board. And so the Mil Mi-10 came into being. In fact the Mi-10 would come in two varieties, the daddy-long-leg Mi-10 and the daddy-short-leg Mi-10K. I have no idea at all what the 'K' meant, but maybe it had something to do with men's trouser leg lengths in the USSR.

The Mi-10 developed out of the Mi-6 flying crane, which had given the Soviet Union the ability to lift and move large and heavy loads with precision. The Mi-6 had two limitations, firstly the size of payload possible, and secondly restrictions on viewing the load when lowering it into the final position. The Mi-10 was designed to resolve these issues, and in addition to a capacity for twenty-eight passengers inside the body, it could carry 3,000kg inside the fuselage, and up to a total of 23,000kg on a suspended platform lashed to the outside of the fuselage and on a sling system – useful for shifting the odd Baltic State or two a few kilometres nearer Moscow.

The first flight took place in June 1959, but suffered a setback with a fatal crash in May 1960. After joining the test programme the second prototype began a series of world-record payload/altitude records for turbine-powered helicopters. Between 1964 and 1969 a total of forty of the long-legged versions entered service.

Crew	4 or 5 (pilot, co-pilot, flight engineer, navigator, technician
Capacity	28 passengers or
	3,000kg internally + 15,000kg on platform +
	8,000kg slung underneath
Length	32.86m (107ft 10in)
Rotor diameter	35m (114ft 10in)
Weight empty	27,100kg (59,620lb)
Gross weight	43,550kg (95,810lb)
Engines	2 x Soloviev D-25V turboshaft engines
Power	4,100kW (5,498hp) each
Cruising speed	180kph
Max speed	335kph
Range	430km
Service ceiling	4,750m
Number built	55

Mil Mi-10.

VERTOL VZ-2

WAS IT INSPIRED BY A DRAGONFLY?

With its skeletal body, and bulbous 'head', the Vertol VZ-2 certainly possesses scary insect-like qualities. Like its near contemporary, the disastrous Hiller X-18, the Vertol was designed to investigate the tilt-wing approach to vertical take-off and landing.

The aircraft had a fuselage made up of a tubular space frame, which initially was left completely uncovered apart from the 'pod' for the pilot. The tail incorporated small ducted fans to assist

Vertol VZ–2.

Crew	1
Capacity	1 passenger/observer
Length	8.05m (26ft 5in)
Rotor diameter	2.9m (9ft 6in)
Wingspan	7.59m (24ft 11in)
Height	4.57m (15ft 0in)
Weight empty	1,678kg (3,692lb)
Engine	1 x Avco Lycoming YT53-L-1 turboshaft
Power	522kW (700hp)
Max speed	340kph
Range	210km
Service ceiling	4,200m
Number built	1

in manoeuvrability at low speeds and when hovering. Ground testing began in April 1957, two years ahead of the Hiller, and a few months later it flew for the first time in hover mode. When the test programme was completed in 1965 the VZ-2 had completed 450 flights in total, of which thirty-four included a full transition from vertical take-off to horizontal flight.

Only one was built, and this is now preserved by NASA. Compared to the Hiller, the VZ-2 was basically quite successful.

Although intrinsically safer than a helicopter, in the sense that aircraft like the VZ-2 and Hiller can glide if the engines fail, the tilt wing idea has never really caught on, possibly on the grounds of cost and complexity.

LOCKHEED XFV SALMON

YET ANOTHER UNSUCCESSFUL EXCURSION INTO THE WORLD OF VTOL

During the 1950s the military aviation world, especially in the US, seemed preoccupied with the idea of vertical take-off and landing (VTOL) combined with normal winged flight in between. The Lockheed XFV falls into the category of 'tail sitters'. It was often called the 'Salmon', after Lockheed's chief test pilot Herman 'Fish' Salmon. It had been planned as a fighter for protecting convoys, and to be based on platforms on conventional ships rather than aircraft carriers.

Initially Lockheed and Convair were approached to tender for the contract, but in 1950 the requirement was changed to one for research aircraft that might later evolve into the ship-based fighter. So in 1951 prototype research aircraft were ordered from both Lockheed and Convair, who would develop their Convair XFY 'Pogo'.

The XFV looked ungainly on the ground, perched on its 'X' shaped tail. However, in reality, it would never be seen like this during its active life. To begin flight testing a temporary undercarriage was fitted using very long braced V-legs at the front and small wheels on the lower two sections of the tail fin.

In many ways the VTOL concept was handicapped by the necessity for the engine to generate more thrust than the weight of the aircraft, a more rigorous requirement than for normal fixed-wing aircraft. In the case of the XFV the designers had wanted the 7,100shp Allison YT-40-A-14 turboprop engine, but this was not yet available, so they had to make do with a 5,332shp Allison XT-40-A-14 unit instead. As it turned out this wasn't really up to the

Crew	1
Length	11.23m (36ft 10in)
Wingspan	8.36m (27ft 5in)
Height	11.23m (36ft 10in)
Weight empty	5,261kg (11,574lb)
Engine	1 x Allison XT40-A-14 turboprop
Power	3,969kW (5,322shp)
Cruising speed	660kph
Max speed	930kph
Range	unknown
Service ceiling	13,100m
Armament	4 x 20mm cannon or 48 x 70mm rockets
Number built	1 + 1 unfinished

job, and whilst a few transitions from horizontal to vertical were achieved in the air, during thirty-two test flights no vertical take-off or landing was undertaken.

By 1955 it had become apparent that the performance of the XFV would never be able to match that of more conventional fighters, and the project was terminated.

Lockheed XFV.

KAMOV KA-56 FOLDING HELICOPTER

THE HELICOPTER YOU COULD TAKE ON HOLIDAY

The Kamov Design Bureau started designing helicopters in 1946. Their first model, the Ka-8, was the earliest single-seat helicopter produced in the Soviet Union. It was powered by a 38hp motorcycle engine, and earned the nickname 'Sky Motorcycle'.

Following the successful demonstration flight of the Ka-8, the designer Nikolai Kamov was asked to design a new helicopter for the Soviet Navy. The Ka-10 was powered by a specially designed lightweight piston engine from Ivchenko, and ten were delivered.

In 1971 the Kamov Design Bureau received a further commission from the Soviet government, this time for a new ultra-lightweight helicopter, the Ka-56, which could be transported in a container of just 500mm diameter. The idea was that the folded helicopter could be carried in a submarine's torpedo tubes. The requirement was that the helicopter could be fully assembled and ready for flight in less than fifteen minutes. The engine was a 40hp air-cooled radial running on ordinary petrol.

The only detachable parts were the rotors, the rest folding neatly into the container. One prototype was built, and it was found that assembly took less than ten minutes. It weighed 220kg ready for take-off, and the helicopter was designed for a top speed of 110kph and a range of 150km.

Unfortunately the Ka-56 never actually flew.

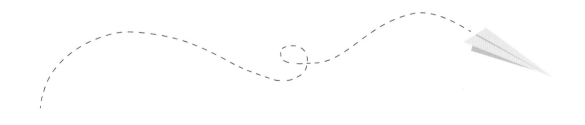

PIASECKI VZ-8 AIRGEEP

AN 'AIRCRAFT' THAT RESEMBLES TWO FLYMOS MATING

The VZ-8 Airgeep was designed to be smaller and easier to fly than a helicopter but marginally more difficult to control than a Flymo. It certainly looked like nothing that had come before, or anything that came after. In essence the Airgeep was two large ducted fans in tandem joined together by a small space for the crew of two. From the side it somewhat resembled a carpet slipper on wheels.

Crew	2 pilot + co-pilot
Capacity	3 passengers
Length	7.45m (24ft 5in)
Rotor diameter	2.5m
Width	2.82m (9ft 3in)
Height	1.78m (5ft 10in)
Weight empty	1,184kg (2,605lb)
Gross weight	1,665kg (3,663lb)
Engine	Garrett AIResearch TPE331-6
Power	410kW (550hp) each
Cruising speed	112kph (70mph)
Max speed	136kph (85mph)
Range	56km (35 miles)
Service ceiling	914m (2,999ft)
Number built	2

It was powered by two 425hp (317kW) Lycoming O-360-A2A piston engines driving the fans through a central gearbox. The first of two ordered by the US Army flew for the first time in September 1958. It was subsequently re-engined with a single 425hp (317kW) Turbomeca Artouste IIB turboshaft, fitted with floats, and loaned to the Navy. On return to the Army a lighter and more powerful 550hp (410kW) Garrett AIResearch TPE331-6 engine was fitted.

A second prototype followed to a much-modified design, including two Artouste engines, ejector seats for the pilot and co-pilot/gunner, and seats for three passengers (who rather perversely didn't have ejector seats, so presumably prior to a crash they would remain strapped in whilst they watched the crew descend gently to safety). The second prototype also included a powered tricycle undercarriage so it could indeed drive around like a Jeep.

While the Airgeep was really intended to fly close to the ground, it was capable of ascending to several thousand feet in the hands of a brave enough pilot, and proved amazingly stable. Very low flying was intended to allow the Airgeep to fly under enemy radar. However, in spite of many advantages over types of craft evaluated by the US Army, the Airgeep programme was terminated in favour of more conventional helicopters.

Piasecki VZ-8 Airgeep.

BELL BOEING V-22 OSPREY

WAS IT TOO CLEVER FOR ITS OWN GOOD?

The Osprey was the first tilt-rotor aircraft developed for military use. It was designed to combine the functionality of a conventional helicopter with that of a long-range high-speed turboprop aircraft.

The joint Bell Boeing helicopter team were awarded the contract in 1983 for a tilt-rotor aircraft, but it would take until 2005 to enter full production. The result was that the original development budget of $2.5 billion grew to a projected $30 billion by 1988, and it was estimated that upwards of $54 billion would be needed to enter full production, an overspend of some twenty times, which may be a record.

In order to meet the design specifications, including the US Navy's requirement that the Osprey could be 'folded up' as shown in the first photograph, the aircraft was exceedingly complex. As a result it proved a

Osprey Tilt Rotor.

Crew	4
Capacity	24 troops seated, 32 maximum
Length	17.5m (57ft 4in)
Wingspan	14m (45ft 10in)
Rotor diameter	11.6m (38ft 0in)
Total gross width	25.8m (84ft 7in)
Weight empty	15,032kg (33,140lb)
Weight loaded	21,500kg (47,500lb)
Engines	2 x Rolls-Royce Alison T406
Power	4,590kW (6,150hp) each
Cruising speed	446kph (277mph)
Max speed	509kph (316mph)
Range	1,627km (1,011 miles)
Armament	2 x 7.62mm machine guns
Number built	458

Osprey Tilt Rotor.

very dangerous beast to operate. The design incorporated separate engines in each wing but driving through a common central gearbox so that if one engine failed the remaining one could drive both rotors. But if the gearbox failed, which was actually more likely than both engines failing, all lift was lost. Whilst technically capable of autorotation like a helicopter, it performed badly under such conditions and the Pentagon's Director of Testing stated that engine failure below 490m (1,600ft) would almost certainly prove fatal.

In addition it would be impossible for the Osprey to glide to a powerless landing under loss of power from a forward flight as the rotor extended below the undercarriage, guaranteeing the craft would roll over forward on landing when the rotors dug into the ground.

Furthermore in naval operation it was found that the heat from the engines could damage the flight decks of the carriers, and it became necessary to place temporary heat shields underneath.

The Osprey's safety record has not been good. During testing from 1991 to 2000 there were four crashes resulting in thirty fatalities, and since becoming operational in 2007 three more fatal crashes due to mechanical problems. The second photograph might suggest the passengers have suddenly learned about the safety record and decided to jump!

Maybe the Osprey was trying to be too many things to too many people.

SIKORSKY S-64 SKYCRANE

HELICOPTERS THAT HAVE BEEN 'CHRISTENED'

When you go to the fishmonger to buy a fish, and ask for it to be gutted, but for the head to be left on, it ends up looking rather like the Sikorsky Skycrane. The Skycrane looks as though an enormous aeronautical fishmonger has ripped its guts out ready for a giant barbecue.

In fact the Skycrane is a clever design giving great flexibility in the heavy-lift helicopter sector. It is an enlarged civilian version of the prototype flying crane helicopter, the S-60. It first flew in 1962, and was sold in seven variants. In 1992 the type certificate and manufacturing rights were bought from Sikorsky by Erickson Air-Crane, who rather delightfully give a name to each S-64, including 'Elvis', 'The Incredible Hulk' and 'Isabelle' used for firefighting in Australia. In addition to firefighting, where it can be fitted with a 10,000-litre tank for fire retardant, S-64s have seen duty in heavy-lift construction, timber harvesting, civil protection, and one, called 'Olga', even hoisted the very top part of the CN Tower in Toronto into place.

Crew	3
Capacity	5 in total including crew
Length	21.41m (70ft 3in)
Rotor diameter	21.95m (72ft 0in)
Weight empty	8,724kg (19,234lb)
Max weight	19,050kg (42,000lb)
Engines	2 x (Pratt & Whitney JFTD12-4A turboshaft
Power	3,555kW (4,500shp) each
Max speed	203kph (126mph)
Range	370km (230 miles)

Sikorsky Skycrane CH-54B.

STRANGE GOINGS-ON ON THE WATER

When aircraft and the sea get together, the results can be very strange indeed. Among the beauties included here are:

- A folding aircraft designed to operate from a submarine, although the 'tickets' may have been strictly one-way.
- An aircraft that goes waterskiing, literally.
- One aircraft so hideously ugly it could induce nightmares.
- Another that can scoop up seawater at 1 tonne per second at 130mph to go fighting forest fires.
- One that normally flies at the dizzying altitude of around 3m.

I suppose the great flying boats, such as the Short S23 'Empire' Flying Boat, could have been included as rather strange, but in a most delightful way. In the 1930s the Imperial Airways flying boat service from the Medway to Cape Town took twelve days, and each evening the aircraft would land in some calm harbour and all the guests would dress formally for dinner. I could certainly live happily with that type of strangeness!

Some of the planes that could have been included in this section have been covered elsewhere; for example the Hughes Hercules and Saunders Roe Princess, which qualified on the 'simply awesome' criterion.

Maybe the only thing missing is an aircraft that can fly both above and below the water surface. Of course that is a ludicrous idea, which could never happen, but then again …

BARTINI BERIEV VVA-14

WAS THIS THE MOST HIDEOUS AIRCRAFT EVER BUILT?

The Bartini Beriev VVA-14 must rank as one of the greatest victories of reality over ambition. The VVA part of its name is an abbreviation for some Russian which means 'vertical take off amphibious aircraft'. It was designed to be able to take off vertically from the water, fly at high speed over long distances, either at high altitude or just skimming the water's surface using ground effect, and then destroy the US Navy's Polaris Submarines … and that just before lunch.

So what went wrong? Well, amongst other things:

- It was originally intended to float on inflatable pontoons which could be collapsed for high-speed flight. However, these caused so many problems that they were replaced by rigid pontoons, giving the ungainly appearance seen in the photograph (only the wings are missing from this surviving prototype). The enormous rigid pontoons ruined high-speed performance.
- The craft was meant to take off vertically using a battery of no fewer than twelve RD-36-35PR turbojets. But these engines never materialised so no vertical take-off was ever achieved.
- Early calculations showed that even the twelve engines would have trouble raising the leviathan out of the water, so two 'starting engines' were installed to blast air into the cavity between the pontoons. But since the main lift engines were never delivered, the starting engines were pointless.
- It was meant to have fly-by-wire capability, but in the end all it got was fly-by-the-seat-of-the-pants capability.
- It was so pig ugly that it is rumoured most people who caught sight of it suffered sleepless nights and nightmares for weeks afterwards.

Crew	3
Length	25.97m (85ft 2in)
Wingspan	30m (98ft 5in)
Height	6.79m (22ft 3in)
Weight empty	23,236kg (51,119lb)
Gross weight	52,000kg (114,400lb)
Engines	2 x D-30M turbofans (for cruising)
	12x RD-36-35 PR turbojets (for lifting)
Power	67kN (15,062lbf) each (cruise engines)
	43kN (9,667lbf) each (lift engines)
Cruising speed	640kph (398mph)
Max speed	760kph (472mph)
Range	2,450km (1,522 miles)
Service ceiling	10,000m (32,800ft)
Number built	2

Bartini Beriev.

DORNIER DO X

THE PASSENGERS MOVED FROM SIDE TO SIDE TO ASSIST BANKING

The Dornier Do X was, when it was built in 1929, the largest, heaviest and most powerful flying boat the world had ever seen. Unfortunately it would also turn out to be a flying boat that nobody actually wanted, which was a tad awkward for Dornier.

The Dornier Do X was financed by the German Transport Ministry, but in order to get around the restrictions on the German aviation industry following the First World War, it was actually built in Switzerland.

Beside the fact that the X resembled a cross between a submarine and a block of flats, the most extraordinary feature was without doubt the motive power. It had no fewer than twelve engines, arranged in six pairs back-to-back, one engine with a tractor propeller and its fellow engine with a pusher propeller. Initially Siemens-built Bristol Jupiter radial engines were fitted, but these proved capable of lifting the X to an altitude of just 425m (1,400ft), deemed not high enough for crossing

Crew	10–14
Capacity	66–100 passengers
Length	40m (131ft 4in)
Wingspan	48m (157ft 5in)
Weight empty	28,250kg (62,280lb)
Weight loaded	56,000kg (123,460lb)
Engines	12 x Curtis Conqueror V12
Power	455kw (610hp) each
Cruising speed	175kph (109mph)
Max speed	211kph (131mph)
Range	1,700km (1,056 miles)
Ceiling	3,200m (10,498ft)
Number built	3

Dornier Do X.

the Atlantic. After completing 103 test flights it was fitted with more powerful Curtiss V-1570 Conqueror V12 cylinder units, which allowed the leviathan to attain the necessary 500m (1,650ft).

Another amazing feature was the level of luxury planned for the passengers, which was almost on a par with transatlantic liners of the day. On the main deck was a smoking room with its own wet bar, a dining room and lounge seating for sixty-six passengers, which could be converted into sleeping berths at night. The cockpit, navigational office, engine control room and radio room were on the upper deck.

The first test flight was in July 1929, but after sixty-nine test flights the seventieth was turned into an 'event' to silence sceptics. On 21 October 1929 it took off with a record load of 169 people, 10 crew, 150 passengers and 9 stowaways without tickets. This record would remain unbroken for twenty years. With the excessive load the X only attained an altitude of 200m (650ft) and to help the seaplane bank and turn the passengers were requested to move from one side to the other, not something that would have gone down well in service!

Just three were built. One remained in Germany but never saw commercial service and eventually ended up in a museum, which was destroyed by the RAF in 1943. The other two went to Italy, but again saw no commercial service and were broken up in 1937.

A record-breaking aircraft in many ways, but one which nobody really wanted.

SIKORSKY S-38

ALSO KNOWN AS THE 'FLYING YACHT'

The S-38 probably doesn't really belong in a book about unusual aircraft, as it really was quite normal and sensible, and sold in considerable numbers. It was more the way it was used which made it 'different'.

The nickname 'Flying Yacht' is a clue. Not only did the fuselage bear more than a passing resemblance to a yacht hull but it was also used by the rich and famous in the same way an expensive yacht might be. Thereby it gained a certain notoriety.

Amongst its famous owners were:

- Howard Hughes, whose ownership alone is enough to make any aircraft unusual.
- Charles Lindbergh, who with his wife Anne Morrow Lindbergh surveyed commercial air routes for Pan Am.
- Robert R. McCormick, newspaper magnate who surveyed commercial air routes across the Atlantic.
- John Hay Whitney, the venture capitalist, who used it as his luxury transport.
- The Flying Hutchinsons, who attempted the first round-the-world flight by a family.
- Filmmakers Martin and Osa Johnson, who explored Africa in the zebra-striped 'Osa's Ark' (in the

Crew	2
Capacity	10 passengers
Length	12.27m (40ft 3in)
Wingspan	21.85m (71ft 8in)
Weight empty	2,727kg (6,000lb)
Weight loaded	4,764kg (10,480lb)
Engines	2 x Pratt & Whitney R-1340 Wasp radial
Power	298kW (400hp) each
Max speed	192kph (120mph)
Range	1,200km (750 miles)
Ceiling	4,878m (16,000ft)
Number built	101

Sikorsky S-38 'Osa's Ark'.

photograph) with companion giraffe-patterned S-39 making safari movies.

In addition it was owned by serveral other famous people who, after they had taken off, were never seen again.

It was also used by twenty-five small (today we would call them boutique) airlines to carry their wealthy clientele.

BERIEV BE-200 SEAPLANE

STRANGE, YES ... BUT DAMNED CLEVER!

The Beriev Be-200 is unique, extremely specialised and a design of almost unparalleled cleverness.

Its specialised roles include firefighting by dropping seawater on the fire, search and rescue, and maritime patrol. But it is in the firefighting role that it excels. It is not unique in being able to scoop up water in flight, as many helicopters have been used to lower enormous canvas 'buckets' into the sea to take water to fires. However, it is the only jet-engined firefighting plane that can scoop at nearly 130mph, taking on 12 tonnes of water in fourteen seconds through four scoops, as it is doing in the photograph. The engines are mounted high up to prevent the ingress of salt water.

In addition to firefighting, it can be configured as a seventy-two passenger plane, an air ambulance for thirty stretcher patients and seven seated patients, whilst for search and rescue it can be equipped with searchlights, sensors, an inflatable boat, thermal and optical surveillance systems, and medical equipment. It is indeed a flexible workhorse.

The Be-200 was designed by the Beriev Aviation Company in collaboration with the Irkutsk Aircraft Production Association. Both companies are now part of the state-owned United Aircraft Corporation. The first flight was completed in September 1998, and the first take-off from water was undertaken in 1999. Production started in 2003, and nine are scheduled for completion.

The Be-200 can operate either from a 1,600m runway on land or from a stretch of open water of at least 2,300m with waves less than 1.3m high.

Beriev Be-200.

Crew	2
Length	32.0m (105ft 0in)
Wingspan	32.8m (107ft 7in)
Height	8.9m (29ft 2in)
Weight empty	27,600kg (60,850lb)
Max take-off weight	41,000kg (90,390lb) from land
	37,900kg (83,550lb) from water
Engines	2 x Progress D-436TP turbofans
Power	73.5kN (16,500lbf) each
Cruising speed	560kph (398mph)
Max speed	700kph (435mph)
Landing speed	200kph (124mph) same for water pick-up
Range	2,100km (1,305 miles)
Service ceiling	8,000m (26,246ft)
Number built	9

ALEKSEYEV A-90 ORLYONOK

THE LITTLE COUSIN OF THE CASPIAN SEA MONSTER

The A-90 Orlyonok is, like the Caspian Sea Monster, an 'ekranoplan', or ground-effect aircraft, but developed a few years later. In fact the Orlyonok was designed not only to skim across the water using ground effect but also to be able to fly like a normal aircraft to altitudes of 3,000m (9,800ft). To this end it had more normal wings than the earlier craft. Also the Orlyonok was amphibious, being equipped with wheels to allow land-based take-offs.

Crew	6
Capacity	150 personnel
Length	58.1m (190ft 7in)
Wingspan	31.5m (103ft 4in)
Height	16.3m (53ft 5in)
Max take-off weight	140,000kg (308,647lb)
Engines	1 x Kuznetsov NK-12-MK turboprop
	2 x Kuznetsov NK-8-4K turbofan
Power	152kN (34,171lbf) turboprop
	103kN (23,155lbf) each turbofans
Cruising speed	400kph (248.5mph)
Range	1,500km (932 miles)
Service ceiling	3,000m (9,842ft)
Armament	2 x 12.7mm machine gun in twin dorsal turret
Number built	5

The other major difference with the Orlyonok was that the main source of propulsion was twin propellers, high up in the tail, and driven by a massive Kuznetsov NK-12 turboprop, the most powerful turboprop ever made. In addition to the turboprop, there were two turbofan engines mounted near the nose, the thrust from which was channelled under the wings to produce extra lift until the forward speed was sufficient to maintain the ground effect. Once under way the front engines could be turned off, avoiding any risk of damage from salt water or sea birds.

Both take-off and landing were also assisted by giant flaps extending the full width of the wings, which captured the thrust from the turbofans as well as directing air from the forward motion downwards. Landings on water were also assisted by a hydro-ski that could be extended out of the belly of the aircraft below the main wings. The whole front of the craft could hinge open to enable speedy disembarkation of troops or a BTR armoured personnel carrier.

Only five Orlyonoks were built, one as a non-flying test unit. Of the other four, two crashed and two remain after being retired in 1993, one on permanent display on the river in Moscow opposite the River Cruise Terminal.

Alekseyev A-90 Orlyonok.

CONVAIR F2Y SEA DART

THE WORLD'S FASTEST WATERSKI

The Convair F2Y is highly significant in two ways. Firstly it is the only seaplane ever to have been planned to exceed the speed of sound. Secondly, and uniquely, it is the only seaplane to ride on waterskis for take-off.

The Sea Dart was Convair's entry into a competition in 1948 for a supersonic interceptor fighter. The US Navy was very cautious about trying to operate supersonic fighters from aircraft carriers because, typically, such aircraft needed very long runways and also had high landing speeds, neither ideal at sea. Convair's suggested solution was to have the aircraft take-off and land on the water. The US Navy clearly warmed to the idea and ordered two prototypes. In fact twelve production aircraft were ordered before the first prototype had even flown.

The Dart was designed with a waterproof hull and two retractable 'waterskis' for take-off and landing. When moving slowly in the water, or when stationary, it floated with the trailing edge of the wing touching the water. During the take-off run air would become trapped under the wing and start to lift the fuselage out of the water. When the plane reached 16kph the skis would start to extend.

Power came from two Westinghouse J34-WE-32 engines, although originally the plan had been to use the more powerful XJ-46-WE-02 turbojets. The air intakes were located high up behind the cockpit to avoid sucking in seawater.

With the lower-powered engines the Sea Dart proved sluggish and could not break the sound barrier, and the death of Convair's chief test pilot in a Convair marked the end of the Sea Dart.

Crew	1
Length	16m (52ft 7in)
Wingspan	10.3m (33ft 8in)
Height	4.9m (16ft 2in)
Weight empty	5,730kg (12,625lb)
Weight loaded	7,480kg (16,500lb)
Engines	2 x Westinghouse J34-WE-32
Power	27kN (6,100lbf) each
Max speed	1,325kph (825mph)
Range	826km (513 miles)
Service ceiling	16,700m (54,800ft)
Armament	4 x 20mm cannon
	Unguided rockets
	2 x air-to-air missiles
Number built	5

Convair F2Y Sea Dart.

AICHI M6A SEIRAN

THE WORLD'S FIRST AND ONLY SUBMARINE-BASED FIGHTER

In spite of looking quite normal, the Aichi Seiran must be a prime candidate for the strangest aircraft of all time. It is the only aircraft ever designed to operate from a submarine. The US Navy had planned to experiment with a sub-based Convair Sea Dart, but decided the technical problems were too great.

From the late 1920s the Japanese Navy had been operating floatplanes from submarines to search for targets. However, the submarine had to remain on the surface until the planes had been dispatched. But in 1941 the Commander-in-Chief of the Navy proposed operating

Crew	2
Length	11.64m (38ft 2in)
Wingspan	12.26m (40ft 2in)
Height	4.58m (15ft 0in)
Weight empty	3,301kg (7,277lb)
Weight loaded	4,040kg (8,907lb)
Engine	1 x Aichi Atsuta Type 31 liquid-cooled inverted V12
Power	1,044kW (1,400hp)
Max speed	474kph (295mph)
Range	1,190km (739 miles)
Service ceiling	9,900m (32,500ft)
Armament	1 x 13mm machine gun
	1 x torpedo or
	2 x 250kg bombs or
	1 x 850kg bomb
Number built	28

Aichi Seiran. (Wikimedia courtesy of Szuyuan huang at the English Language Wikipedia)

Aichi M6A1
Seiran.

aircraft from submarine aircraft carriers in order to launch attacks on the US.

To fulfil this requirement Aichi was requested to design a folding attack aircraft with a range of 1,500km and a speed of 555kph. Developed out of the earlier D4Y1 SuiSei, the final design was for a two-seat, low-winged monoplane powered by a 1,050kW (1,410hp) Aichi AE1P Atsuta 30 engine (actually a version of the Daimler Benz DB601 V12 unit). The plane was designed to fold up sufficiently to fit inside a 3.5m-diameter tubular 'hangar' on the I-400-Class submarines. The hangar was capable of holding three aircraft, which were unfolded and then launched by catapult on the surface. In some cases the aircraft made do without any undercarriage or floats on the basis that the missions would be strictly 'one way'. In any case the chances of a Seiran pilot locating his submarine again, which would be submerged, were virtually nil; Seiran sorties would be essentially suicide missions.

The I-400s and their Aichi Seirans never saw action. It was during the first operational sortie that Japan surrendered, and the two I-400s dumped all their Seirans into the ocean.

IS IT A FRISBEE? IS IT A BOOMERANG?

Some aircraft designers come up with creations that bear more resemblance to a frisbee or a boomerang than to what we commonly think of as an aeroplane. In this last section of the book some of these design freaks are reviewed.

NORTHROP YB-35

THE FLYING WING STRIKES AGAIN

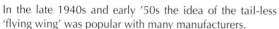

In the late 1940s and early '50s the idea of the tail-less 'flying wing' was popular with many manufacturers.

The Northrop YB-35 was an experimental heavy bomber developed just after the Second World War. It was the personal brainchild of Jack Northrop, who had been advocating the flying wing format as a means of reducing drag and eliminating structural weight not directly contributing to lift. The 1941 request sent out for a

Northrop YB-35.

Crew	9
Length	16.2m (53ft 11in)
Wingspan	52.2m (172ft 0in)
Height	6.2m (20ft 3in)
Weight empty	40,590kg (89,300lb)
Weight loaded	94,802kg (180,000lb)
Engines	2 x Pratt & Whitney R-4360-17 radial
	2 x Pratt & Whitney R-4360-21 radial
Power	2,237kW (3,000hp) each
Max speed	632kph (393mph)
Range	13,100km (8,150 miles)
Service ceiling	12,100m (39,700ft)
Armament	20 x 12.7mm M3 Browning machine guns
	23,210kg (51,070lb) bombs

super-long-range bomber, which resulted in the Convair B-36, was extended to include Northrop.

However, the development of the YB-35 was deeply tied up in politics, and misguided mistrust in the more adventurous flying-wing format led to the contract going to Convair with their B-36. The B-36 proved to be extremely expensive and very unreliable, and it might have been very different if the more radical YB-35 solution had been followed. As compensation for not getting the bomber contract, Northrop was given the contract for the F-89 Scorpion fighter, which would be a great success.

WAINFAN FACETMOBILE

AN AMAZING DIY PROJECT

One of the most interesting things about the Wainfan Facetmobile is its name. Wainfan sounds like the technical term for a special type of jet engine: '... oh yes, we tried a turbofan, but a wainfan proved vastly superior.' In fact Wainfan is the delightful family name of two of the three design team, Barnaby Wainfan and Lynne Wainfan. Secondly, Facetmobile. In fact the aircraft consists of eleven flat facets, following the concept of 'stealth technology' seen in the F-117 Nighthawk, although in reality the angular shape is simply the result of covering a space frame with fabric.

All that aside, the Facetmobile has to be just about the ultimate 'lifting body'. The whole thing is simply a low-aspect-ratio wing, a flat, angular lifting surface. The prototype first flew in 1993, and was quite successful in the air. Unfortunately the prototype crashed in 1995 following an engine failure, but the pilot, Barnaby Wainfan, was not injured and the aircraft has been partially repaired but not yet flown again.

As DIY projects go, the Facetmobile is up there with the boldest and most exciting ... and it does have a delightful name!

Crew	1
Length	5.94m (19ft 6in)
Wingspan	4.6m (15ft 0in)
Weight empty	168kg (370lb)
Weight loaded	336kg (740lb)
Engine	1 x Rotax 503 DC
Power	37kW (50hp)
Cruising speed	148kph (92mph)
Max speed	178kph (110mph)

ARUP S1

The Arup S1, also known as the Snyder Glider, was designed by Dr Cloyd Snyder, who, apart from having a most unusual first name, was a practising podiatrist in Indiana. Maybe day after day of treating feet had a profound effect on his mind, because he suddenly decided to build aircraft.

In fact his inspiration did come from his foot work. He idly tossed a felt heel lift through the air one day, as one does, and was intrigued to find it generated some lift. The S1 was the first in a series of so-called 'heel lift' vehicles he designed. At first the S1 was a pure glider, but later he fitted a motorcycle engine, and it and its successors, especially the S2 and S4, were remarkably successful and accident free.

Snyder had envisaged taking the ideas further, even as far as a craft with wings 15ft thick and partly filled with helium for extra lift. The passengers would be accommodated inside the wing with a forward view through a transparent section. However, Snyder lacked the working capital and business expertise to take the ideas further.

Oh, by the way, the name 'Arup' has nothing to do with the well-known civil engineering company ... it is short for 'Air up'. I suppose if Snyder had been a podiatrist in Lancashire he'd have called it the 'Eh up'.

Arup S1.

Crew	1
Length	4.3m (14ft 1in)
Wingspan	6.1m (20ft 0in)
Engine	1 x Heath Henderson B-4
Power	19kW (26hp)
Max speed	977kph (607mph)
Number built	1

NORTHROP N-1M

ALSO KNOW AS THE 'JEEP' ... WHY?

The Northrop N-1M acquired the nickname 'Jeep', although for the life of me I cannot imagine why. It looks as much like a jeep as I look like George Clooney.

Jack Northrop had been interested in the flying-wing concept since the 1920s. His first experimental aircraft using this idea was the 1929 Flying Wing X-216H. However, this had twin booms attached behind the 'flying wing' with twin rudders and a horizontal stabiliser joining the two. So to that extent it wasn't a pure flying wing as such.

The N-1M was one of a series of craft that developed a pure flying-wing idea. In order to allow for easy design 'tweaks' the wing itself was made of laminated wood whilst the main central fuselage into which the wing blended was a tube of steel. It also featured pusher propellers, a favourite of Jack Northrop.

The 'Jeep' first took to the skies in July 1941. In fact the first flight was accidental, as the test pilot had only planned a taxi run. After a few changes to the wing design, the N-1M proved successful but underpowered, so the original Lycoming engines were replaced by larger Franklin units, again buried inside the deep wing.

The N-1M completed a whole series of test flights up until 1945, and paved the way for Northrop's much larger YB-35 and YB-49 aircraft.

Northrop N-1M.

Crew	1
Length	5.46m (17ft 11in)
Wingspan	11.79m (38ft 8in)
Weight loaded	1,769kg (3,900lb)
Engines	2 x Franklin 6AC air-cooled flat-6
Power	87kW (117hp) each
Max speed	322kph (200mph)
Range	483km (300 miles)
Ceiling	1,219m (4,000ft)
Number built	1

NORTHROP YB-49

A SERIOUS 'FLYING WING'!

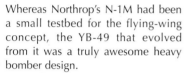

Whereas Northrop's N-1M had been a small testbed for the flying-wing concept, the YB-49 that evolved from it was a truly awesome heavy bomber design.

In fact the two YB-49s built were converted YB-35 test aircraft, which had been powered by radial piston engines. By 1944, with the development of the YB-35 seriously behind schedule, the contract for the propeller-powered flying wing was cancelled. But the USAF continued testing with one YB-35, and then ordered two YB-35s fitted with jet engines instead. The first of these flew in October 1947 and immediately showed more promise than the piston-engined craft. The aircraft actually set an unofficial endurance record, flying above 40,000ft for six and a half hours.

Sadly the YB-49 never entered production, being passed over in favour of the more conventional piston-engined Convair B-36 'Peace-maker', which also features in this book. However, the flying-wing development work would prove valuable to Northrop in the eventual development of the B-2 'stealth bomber' which entered service in the early 1990s. In 1980, when Jack Northrop was elderly and wheelchair bound, he was taken to the Northrop company that he founded and ushered into a classified area where he was shown a scale model of the future B-2. Unable to speak due to illness, he wrote on a pad of paper: 'I now know why God has kept me alive for the last 25 years.' He died ten months later, eight years before the B-2 entered service.

Early jet engines were incredibly 'dirty' under full throttle. The photograph shows one of the YB-49s taking off, and a truly awesome sight (and sound) it was!

Crew	7
Length	16.0m (53ft 1in)
Wingspan	52.4m (172ft 0in)
Weight empty	40,116kg (88,442lb)
Weight loaded	60,581kg (133,559lb)
Engines	6 or 8 x Allison J35-A turbojets
Power	17kN (5,000lbf) each
Max speed	793kph (495mph)
Range	16,057km (9,978 miles)
Ceiling	13,900m (45,700ft)
Armament	4 x 12.7mm machine guns
	14,500kg (32,000lb) bombs
Number built	2

Northrop YB-49.

A FINAL WORD

Having compiled, and certainly enjoyed writing, this book, I now reflect on the possibility of the ultimate strange airborne vehicle, or, since the aviation world seems to like abbreviations and nicknames, what I will call the USAV or 'Monty Python' plane.

Judging from what I have seen designers have put into the air in the past, the USAV would have the following characteristics:

- Have one hundred 'winglets'.
- Possess the ability to be folded up and stored in a suitcase, and weigh no more than 2kg.
- Be largely solar powered.
- Be able to fly anywhere between 2m (ground effect) to 50,000m (sub-space) in altitude.
- Be capable of Mach 3 but also able to hover.
- Be completely asymmetrical in order to be 'interesting'.
- Be driveable on normal roads at up to 150mph.
- Be able to fly underwater like a submarine.
- Be capable of carrying 300 passengers in supreme luxury, each having a bedroom, sitting room, bathroom and study.
- Look so cute it could become an instant bestselling soft toy called Percy the Plane.
- Be instantly and totally biodegradable within fifteen seconds of the end of its service life.
- Cost the same as a small family car.

Of course all this is completely far-fetched, and fanciful nonsense. But didn't they say the same thing about the earliest aircraft?

I suspect the only obstacle to the USAV becoming reality is money … I think this book demonstrates that the designers certainly don't lack the imagination!

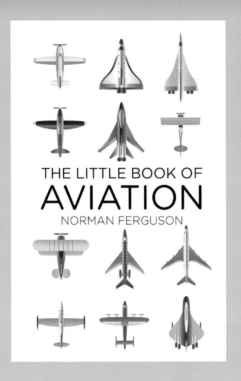

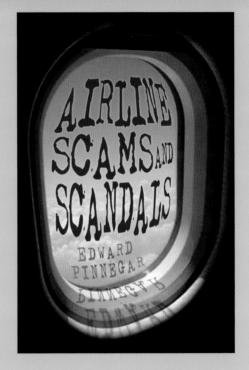

The Little Book of Aviation

NORMAN FERGUSON

ISBN 978 0 7524 8837 0

Airline Scams and Scandals

EDWARD PINNEGAR

ISBN 978 0 7524 6625 5